Nineteen hundred and ninety-two is a year that means a lot to Spain, for it marks the five hundredth anniversary of that great event that extended the limits of the world.

And it is within this perspective that Barcelona is presenting its candidature for selection as the seat of the Olympic Games of the 25th Olympiad, the Olympic Games of 1992.

While personally, as an Olympic sportsman – for I took part in the Munich Games, the nautical events of which were held in Kiel – I am moved at the thought of my country organizing Olympic Games, as King of Spain I must proclaim my pride that in 1992, five hundred years after the discovery of America, the eyes of the world should again be fixed on what is happening in a city in our country – and that city one in which, as I am well aware, the Olympic spirit of universal friendship and brotherhood is kept very much alive.

I can confidently declare that, if Barcelona is honoured with the task of organizing the Olympic Games of 1992, the young people of the whole world will find in Spain that atmosphere of friendship and freedom, faith in the future and solidarity without distinction of race, religion or political ideas, that is so clearly identified with the Olympic ideals and principles.

Juan Carlos I
King of Spain

I

As Mayor of Barcelona and the representative a community with an ardent desire to be the host-city for the XXV Olympiad of 1992. I have great pleasure in presenting this book, which will serve as an important point of reference when the moment arrives to implement the Candidature of Barcelona.

The text is a summary of the preliminary project presented by the Candidature of Barcelona to the Spanish Olympic Committee and to the Spanish Government and it is designed to bring out the most important aspects of our proposal. I would like this documentation to be distributed among the whole international Olympic family with the hope that the efficiency and effort of all the institutions, entities and people involved in promoting the Barcelona project will be appreciated and welcomed.

This summary is an expression of the capability and hopes of a whole nation with a view to the staging of the XXV Olympic Games and also of the wish of this nation to deepen the friendship in Mankind through sport.

I trust you will find this book interesting and that you will be in a position to appreciate the possibilities offered by Barcelona for the 1992 Summer Olympics.

Pascual Maragall
Mayor of Barcelona

BARCELONA
IN CONTEMPORARY SPAIN

When Spain was rediscovered by the French, English, and German romanticists at the end of the eighteenth century and the beginning of the nineteenth century, it was a remote, curious country, full of exotic colour, which pleased foreigners but worried those who were native to the land because of its backwardness. In the nineteenth century and the first half of the twentieth the country made a great effort to become modernized, especially in Catalonia and the Basque country, and it became evident that modernization was perfectly feasible. The inferiority complex with respect to the more advanced regions of the world persisted, however, and became even more pronounced over the long postwar period in spite of the fact that it was in the nineteen fifties and especially in the nineteen sixties that Spain experienced an upsurge in its economy and a change in its mentality in the country as a whole and in some areas in particular, just as was happening in the rest of the industrialized world.

Nevertheless, it was only with the advent of democracy in 1977 that the country was relieved, almost overnight, of the sensation of being ten, twenty or even a hundred years behind the rest of Europe as had been the belief up to that time. This self confidence was of paramount importance in the modernization of the general state structures in spite of the serious economic recession which began in 1973. The prospect of Spain's joining the Common Market or more palpable events such as holding the International Exhibition in Seville and the Olympic Games in Barcelona, have given much encouragement for the reconstruction, restoration, recreation and reshaping of a country which has become fully integrated in the so called age of post-industrial modernity but which has not lost what it has traditionally been over the centuries.

It would appear quite evident that Spain is not destined to be a great power at the end of this century or the next. This is no disadvantage, however. The category of "second-class" country would seem to be quite convenient. The "aurea mediocritas", of the Greeks and the Romans, i.e. the balance between the two opposite poles of wealth and poverty, of militarism and impotence, of aimless avant-gardism and backwardness with no future, appears to be be symbolized in a community like Spain, which has already had the experience of being the first world power, in the period of the discovery of America, and also of the sufferings of being a Third World type country before and after that age of glory.

Spain also occupies a privileged position. When one travels around the world one realizes the prestige Europe, and in particular the Mediterranean, still has. Most countries, including the all powerful North America, take delight in this ancient corner of the world where the cultural civilization which still governs the destiny of the globe was born. Spain is located in the best position between the Mediterranean and Europe to favour and potentiate relations with the New World, with the World of the future, the "Americas", which sooner or later will awaken from their sleep.

In recent years the idea of linear, uninterrupted progress has been shown to be either a fallacy or a drawback. Therefore, a country like Spain which still has many traditions —as can be seen, for example, by the fact that there are four official languages– which are kept alive in many different ways, but which is a country "condemned" to progress both materially and culturally, becomes a modern country without harshness and a traditional country without drawbacks.

The present-day, increasingly decentralized Spanish State with its autonomous regions ensures both variety and the singular outstanding nature of each of the regions and nationalities which make up the State. Castile is now able to recover its beautiful medieval cities and its splendid culture which flourished in the so called Golden Age, as did other world cultures, with Cervantes, Quevedo, Teresa de Jesús, Juan de la Cruz, or Calderón, to mention but a few of the great writers of the time.

Andalusia, the region with the oldest culture in Spain and perhaps in Europe, is beginning to recover its traditional identity, a mixture of prehistoric, Roman, Christian, and Moorish culture, and is becoming a new region full of creative spirit and great artists, such as Góngora, Velázquez or García Lorca were in the past.

Similar things are happening in other regions of Spain not so famous outside the country, such as Aragón, Navarra, Asturias, León, Extremadura, Murcia, País Valenciano, the Canary Islands, or the Balearic Islands, each of which has special individual features which make the area stand out between tradition and modernity, such as winter tourism in the Canary Islands, summer tourism in the Balearic Islands, and in all the regions in general the countryside, gastronomy, agriculture, livestock breeding, and industry, not forgetting all the different cultural hues.

The ancient nations of Galicia, the Basque country, and Catalonia, more or less integrated in the last centuries in the Spanish State, but quite removed from a single national integration, have many special features, especially in the case of Catalonia and Euzkadi (the Basque country) because of their century-long process of adaptation to Europe in the fields of trade, industry, and culture. Galicia is perhaps more isolated and relates more, by virtue of language and tradition, to Portugal and Brazil, in the same way as the rest of Spain relates to Latin America.

Madrid is the capital of the Spanish state and the "breakwater of the many regions which make up Spain". It is a lively, agile city owing to its tradition, its central location, and its new role as a powerful trade, industrial, financial, and cultural centre, which makes it one of the most important cities in Europe.

The present situation inspires a high degree of optimism when one considers the deep-rooted, soul destroying pessimism which prevailed until just a few years ago. This optimism is mitigated, however, by the economic recession, which is particularly pronounced in the most industrialized areas. Nevertheless, an overall idea is obtained of this "miniature continent" known as Spain, which is very varied in its countryside, culture and ethnic qualities. The country progresses more every day towards a harmonious balance by fitting together its different pieces in a rational, democratic, and active manner, just as very different countries such as Italy,

Germany, Switzerland, and the United States have done. Spain is endeavouring to overcome its financial and social differences by implementing a policy of justice beneficial to the country as a whole and to everyone who lives in it.

There is no doubt that Spain has not yet been fully exploited and just one example will confirm this. It is the common and justified opinion that the towns and cities of Italy are the most beautiful in the world. While we are not claiming that Spanish cities can match those in Italy on an overall basis, many of our towns and cities could be extremely attractive if they were properly restored. Think, for example, of the towns and cities of Andalusia where Moorish architecture is combined with popular tradition. Think of the Romanesque churches and villages in the Pyrenees. Remember such exceptional towns and cities as Toledo, Ávila, Salamanca, Cáceres, Sigüenza, Atienza, Toro, or Zamora, not to mention Santiago de Compostela, Oviedo, Burgos, Santander, San Sebastián, Pamplona, and Barbastro, or the towns and villages of Valencia and Murcia. Finally, the coastal towns and resorts of the whole peninsula and the two great archipelagoes are worthy of special mention. In every region of Spain can be found real architectural wonders: castles, churches, ancestral homes, popular dwellings, bridges, and a host of art treasures, all of which have been preserved thanks to the fact that modernity has not managed to exert its destructive influence on them and also because no "world war" has annihilated them. Credit should also be given to local corporations and private individuals who have not allowed the historic monuments and treasures which give their towns flavour and tradition to disappear.

The same could be said of the countryside with its extremely varied vegetation and with more fauna than one could possibly believe.

One could also speak of the different languages, the three Romance languages: Castilian, Catalan, and Galician, or the Basque language which comes into a category all of its own. Also worthy of mention is the incredible folklore of Spain: its dances, festivals, processions, pottery, buildings, folk tales, traditional songs, etc. or the varied gastronomy, which has gradually been discovered over recent years and which has brought pleasure to natives and foreigners alike. It is no wonder that every day more books, magazines, collections of photos and films appear to propagate this endless wealth which acts as a platform for modern culture and arts, which are still not promoted as much as they should be.

Catalonia

If the Iberian Peninsula is like a small continent inside Europe, Catalonia too possesses many varied features which distinguish it from other regions of Spain. It is often said that Catalonia is the union of the mountains with the sea, especially of the Pyrenean districts with the coastal areas; but this implies omitting the lands of the depression of the Ebro, i.e. those areas by which the country relates to the Meseta.

Catalonia can be divided into three large units: the mountainous area, the inland plain, and the coastal region. It therefore has three very different "worlds", the first two being continental, and the third more varied and directly related to the great civilizations of the Mediterranean.

The Pyrenees are a mountain range 200 kilometres in length. The highest peaks —over

3.000 metres– are to be found in the west and the mountains become generally lower towards the east until the range sinks into the sea at the beautiful Cape of Creus. The Pre-Pyreness run parallel to the Pyrenees, with attractive limestone mountains such as the Sierra del Cadí. The Sub-Pyrenees close the Central Lowlands in the north.

The Central Lowlands comprise great dry plains in the region of Lleida and are of a continental nature. They are bordered by the Pyrenees in the north and by the Sierra del Interior in the east.

The Mediterranean range comprises the coast and its small plains opening onto the sea, and the double mountain range which runs parallel to the coast: the Sierra Litoral or the Sierra de Marina, which runs from the French frontier down as far as Garraf and which mostly follows the shoreline, and the Sierra Interior, almost parallel to the Sierra Litoral but which is higher. The Depresión Pre-litoral (lowlands situated before the shoreline), a very important corridor through which people have travelled since time immemorial as is shown by the fact that the main routes still pass through this area. This is also where the majority of the population has settled and where economic activity is very lively, surpassed only by the city of Barcelona in both population and economic activity.

Catalonia has an area of 31,390 square kilometres, 6.3 % of Spanish peninsular territory, although with a population density well above the average for Spain: about 16 % of the whole. Neither is the area of the region proportional to its economic productivity as Catalonia accounts for a quarter of all Spanish industry. The hydrographic network comprises the Ebro and its tributaries in the west, the Ter and the Llobregat, among others, which flow into the Mediterranean in the east, and in the north less important watercourses such as the Garonne, which flows into the French coast. Hydroelectric power, obtained mainly from the western rivers, is one of the few natural resources of Catalonia as the country is rather poor in this respect. Catalonia has to import most of its natural products and the wealth of the country lies in its industrial capacity and commercial power.

For climatic reasons the region may be divided into three areas: alpine and subalpine in the Pyrenees, Atlantic in the Garonne valley, and the Mediterranean. The latter is divided into the mountain region (Pre-Pyrenees, Transversal Range, Montseny), with relatively mild temperatures and a lower rainfall than in the Pyrenees; the Sierra pre-Litoral, where it is hotter; and the Coastline, with hot, dry summers and rainy autumns.

Tradition and the present

It is not necessary here to go back as far as the times when the country was occupied by other peoples previous to the period of Romanization of the peninsula. It should be mentioned, however, that Romanization was carried out in depth in the fields of language and culture, social organization, and economy. Tarraco, Tarragona, was the capital of the peninsula for many years and the main port through which Rome introduced its civilization.

Catalan history as such did not really begin until the time of Charlemagne, around 800, when his armies conquered the lands to the south of the eastern Pyrenees and established a series of shires, such as Barcelona, Girona, Ampúries, Urgell, Osona, and Cerdanya, which depended on the imperial power of the Franks. These shires or counties made up the Hispanic March which enabled the Empire to defend itself from the Moorish invasion by putting land in the way. A century later, Guifred I el Pilós (Wilfred the Hairy) managed to unify these and other lands under his power and Catalonia was thus born. Throughout the Middle Ages and under the auspices of Barcelona, Catalonia became one of the great powers of the Mediterranean, with Barcelona itself as the most powerful city of the Western Mediterranean matching Venice in the Eastern Mediterranean. The Catalans, on their own or later united with the kingdom of Aragón, extended their power to the south of France, to the Roussillon and Cerdanya regions, conquered the Balearic Islands and the lands of Valencia and even overcame Sicily and Sardinia. For a while the Crown of Aragón-Catalonia ruled over the dukedoms of Athens and Neopatria in Greece.

Around the time of the formation of Catalonia, in the ninth century, the Catalan language was born. This language is derived from Latin as is the case with other Romance languages and was used in the conquered lands. In the last two centuries of the Middle Ages the Catalan language boasted many great poets and prose writers, either in Catalonia itself or in other areas where the language was spoken.

In the thirteenth century the kings and queens of the House of Barcelona established a kind of constitutional monarchy, which was among the first in Europe. The Generalitat, the main institution of government, was founded as was also the parliament, which was composed of the nobility, the Church, merchants, and craftsmen.

Catalonia continued to have its statutes and self-government when the kingdom joined that of Castile when Ferdinand of Catalonia and Aragon married Isabella of Castile. Nevertheless, Catalonia gradually lost its power as a result of the wars and plagues of the fifteenth century. The discovery of America brought about a shift in the centre of interest from the Mediterranean to the new lands which had been discovered and monopolized by Castile. The slow process of centralization had begun. The sixteenth, seventeenth and the first part of the eighteenth centuries saw the great decline of Catalonia, which finally resulted in the loss of self-government when the house of Austria was substituted by that of the Bourbons at the beginning of the eighteenth century. Catalonia was invaded by the Castilian troops and absorbed into the Spanish State. The ancient merchant and craftsmen traditions of Catalonia flourished in the second half of the eighteenth century, however, mostly owing to the fact that it was only then that the Catalans were authorized to trade with the American colonies. The population, which had been greatly reduced, gradually increased again and in the third decade of the nineteenth century Catalonia became the most powerful industrial area in Spain. With the economic and cultural rebirth (the *Renaixença*) Catalonia began to aspire to regaining its lost autonomy. Strong nationalist feelings grew up and the Catalan language, which had never been abandoned, acquired literary importance. The region as a whole came to be the driving European force of the peninsula.

At the beginning of the twentieth century Catalonia reached another historical peak, with poets such as Verdaguer and Maragall, novelists such as Narcís Oller and Victor Català, architects such as Antoni Gaudí, Domènech i Montaner, and Puig i Cadafalch (the main elements in the great Modernist movement) and an endless list of businessmen and industrialists, important scientists and large institutions of all kinds, such as travel and sports clubs. At this time Catalonia was one of the most industrialized and modern regions of Europe.

Catalonia reawakened and recovered its self confidence. It achieved a limited form of government known as the Mancomunitat at the beginning of the century and in a moment of cultural euphoria which produced new politicians, great writers such as Carner, d'Ors, Josep Maria de Sagarra, Carles Riba, Josep Pla, Carles Soldevila, Foix, and many others, along with great painters, sculptors, and musicians, who have filled the twentieth century with their works, making this period perhaps the most fertile in the history of Catalonia. Political and social confrontations, sometimes very serious, as in the majority of advanced countries of the time, made life difficult and finally brought about the dictatorship of Primo de Rivera. With the advent of the Second Republic, however, Catalonia recovered its statute of autonomy, although at a time of such political stress that it hardly had time to carry out the necessary reforms and other tasks. The civil war and the subsequent long years of the dictatorship were sad times for Catalonia and for all of Spain. It was only after 1975 that culture recovered its freedom, Catalonia its autonomy, and the political parties their democratic liberty.

At present Catalonia has six million inhabitants. Its surface area and population are similar to those of Denmark or the Netherlands. The population is about 2.3 % of that of the Common Market but while the average annual population increase in the EEC was 0.8 % that of Catalonia was higher, with a figure of 2.3 % between 1950 and 1970 –the years of the "Spanish economic miracle"–, because of many people emigrating to Catalonia from other agricultural areas of Spain. The total population increase in this period was 60 % according to information issued by the Department of Economy and Finance of the Generalitat in 1981. These immigrants found work in the building trade and in industry. The economic growth of Catalonia was thus highly favoured. The problem was, however, that Catalonia could not absorb this influx of immigrants, in part because it was not at liberty to do so and in part because of the large number of immigrants involved. Two communities thus came into being –the Catalan community as such, and the "foreigners". With time and an adequate political policy the two groups gradually fused together.

As is the case with industrialized regions Catalonia is a highly urbanized country. Of the six million inhabitants, over 3 million live in the metropolitan area of Barcelona, which is the main financial, cultural and trade centre not only of Catalonia but also of the whole of Spain. 80 % of the Catalan population lives in communities with over 10,000 inhabitants. These communities are mainly located in the coastal area.

An economy in progress

While the number of people employed in agriculture in Catalonia is similar to that of the Common Market countries and much lower than the rest of Spain (Catalonia: 7 % of the population; EEC 7 %; Spain 20 %), the percentage employed in industry is much higher than the European average (Catalonia: 53 %; EEC 40 %). On the other hand the number employed in the service sector is lower than that of Europe, and even than the rest of Spain (Catalonia: 40 %; Spain: 42 %; EEC: 52 %). This is mainly due to the fact that until the advent of democracy in 1977, Catalonia did not have its own administration to expand the services sector typical of more advanced countries.

The main Catalan agricultural areas are in the Lleida district, in the Ebro Delta and the coastal plains of the Empordà and the Camp de Tarragona. The agricultural operations are usually on a small scale and this is observed in almost all Catalan economic activity. Therefore, agriculturalists should intensify their crops by mechanizing where possible and by carrying out good irrigation programmes. The main crops are those typical of the Mediterranean areas: grapes, olives, and cereals, together with other more productive crops, such as vegetables and fruit.

The woods are not very thick and their yield is very low. Livestock breeding is more important and in combination with poultry breeding accounts for more than fifty per cent of agricultural production.

The industrial revolution began in Catalonia with the textile sector in the eighteenth century. The metallurgical industry followed suit and then the idea was taken up by other sectors. The country is thus in a position to handle an economic crisis like the one it is suffering at present. As has already been mentioned, Catalonia has few natural resources and the wealth of the country lies in the transformation of imported materials.

Of all the industrial sectors the metallurgical industry is the most important and also the most varied. The economic recession which began in 1973 has affected this industry considerably and there is now a need for a thorough reconversion process. The most important sectors are the car industry, with the SEAT company, located in the Zona Franca in Barcelona (this company is the most active); electric motors and machinery; textile machinery and others.

The chemical sector is the most important in Spain with large companies in Barcelona, Tarragona, and Martorell. There are also many large companies manufacturing pharmaceuticals and perfumes, and paints and varnishes.

In spite of having lost some of its fighting power, the textile sector is still of great economic importance and involves all the activities linked to such an industry, from spinning to finishing. Previously the industry dealt mainly with cotton and wool, but now these materials are combined with synthetic fibres.

Other important sectors are the food industry, with wine and spiced sausages as the most important products; the building trade, which in the past was mainly concerned with buildings for private individuals, is now trying to compensate for lack of demand in this sector by concentrating its efforts in the public sector which, with the coming of the Autonomous Government is now more lively; publishing, some of which is in the Catalan language but most of which is in Castilian, covering the Spanish and also the Latin American markets; the paper industry etc.

A country open tot the future

Catalonia has been divided administratively since 1833 into four provinces based on the French state structure: Barcelona, Tarragona, Lleida, and Girona, each of which has its own provincial delegation. The traditional division of the country, however, was based on districts which were established according to geographical and economic divisions and also the historical division, which was recognized in the Statute of Autonomy of 1932. This form of administration was forbidden under the Franco dictatorship but now the division into districts is accepted in a generalized manner. There are 38 separate districts grouped into nine regions with the following capitals: Tremp, Vic, Girona, Lleida, Manresa, Barcelona, Tarragona, Reus, and Tortosa.

In order to know and understand Catalonia, its tourism and its sporting activities, it is of paramount importance to respect these district divisions as they show the real nature of the country. The Pyrenean districts –the Vall d'Aran, the Pallars Sobirà, (Andorra, which has two co-rulers: the President of the French State and the Bishop of the Seu d'Urgell), Cerdanya, Ripollés, Garrotxa, and Alt Empordà, have beautiful valleys, snowy peaks, and "alpine" architecture. They offer good walking and climbing, interesting sightseeing routes (Romanesque churches) and a chance to meet the local inhabitants. The districts of the Girona coastal area –Empordà and La

Selva have attractive lands open to the whole world with the Costa Brava and its rocky terrain overlooking the sea, the small bays and its beautiful beaches, the small coastal villages with their tradition of seafaring people, and first class tourist facilities. In just one of the resorts, Lloret, with ten thousand permanent residents, there is more hotel accomodation than in the whole of Greece. The area also has good marinas and summer entertainment. The districts surrounding Barcelona are a strange and curious mixture of industry and inland or coastal natural surroundings. The area thus appears unique, progressive and avant-garde as the examples given below will show.

Some 40 million tourists come to Spain every year and 12 million of these enter the country through Catalonia. The country offers 334 beaches covering a distance of 268 kilometres; 204 days of sunshine per year; 35 marinas and sailing clubs; 12 ski resorts; 8 golf courses; 308 hunting grounds; 5 natural reserve parks; 145 museums; hotel accomodation for over 800,000 people; camping accomodation for 250,000 people; 3 casinos, and a large variety of sporting and social facilities and cultural institutions, according to information issued by the Department of Economy and Finance of the Generalitat in 1980.

Of the 3,422 sports establishments in Catalonia, 36 % are for football, athletics, and tennis; 32 % for basketball, handball or hockey; 14 % are swimming pools, 15 % are gymnasiums, judo clubs, etc.; and 2 % are for petanca, bowling, etc. Mention should also be made of the long tradition of excursionist clubs. The main institution is the *Centre Excursionista de Catalunya*, which has contributed greatly to spreading knowledge of the country, its folklore and traditions, photography and documentary films, as have equivalent bodies in Germany, France, and Great Britain.

We shall now proceed to look at the most attractive points of various cities and areas, beginning with Barcelona, of which an ample description will be given in the pages which follow. Girona has beautiful churches and a very interesting old quarter, not forgetting the excellent view from the River Onyar. Lleida, on the Segre, the historical Mount of Sura, has ancient religious and civil buildings. Tarragona is the old Roman city which has preserved for 2000 years the praetorium, the forum, the amphitheatre, the splendid walls, and the necropolis. Most of the large and small towns, and many villages too have many archaeological monuments (Ripoll, Montblanch, Terrassa, Balaguer, Figueres, Cardona, etc. etc.). Other coastal tourist attractions, in addition to those already mentioned, are the beaches and villages of the Costa Dorada, between Sitges and the Ebro Delta along with the rice fields and beautiful fauna of the delta itself.

The excellent network of motorways, roads and railways; the seaports and airports all make business and pleasure travel very easy.

BARCELONA

How can one enter into the spirit of such a large, complex city as Barcelona with its two thousand years of history? Personally, what gives me most pleasure is to imagine what the area must have been like before the city itself was born. I would like to go back to two thousand years BC but I also take delight in trying to imagine what Barcelona will be like in the year 2000 AD, which seems to be approaching at lightning speed.

In those ancient Neolithic times, men and women, families, and entire clans passed through the circle of mountains that borders a wide plain opening onto the sea but these people did not stay for long. Nevertheless, at least one small group settled on the slope of the hill of Monterolas and lived and died there. We know this because of a grave discovered in the 1920's when a German was laying the foundations for a house on the corner of Carrer Copernico and Carrer Muntaner. We can imagine a little of what those people must have been able to see from their mountain vantage point: behind them rose the Sierra de Collserola with its highest peak, the Tibidabo; the foothills of the Sierra, like the slope on which they lived, covered with thick oak forests, oak being the tree native to this country; at their feet the plain which descends from the Tibidabo to Catalunya Square, also covered with oaks and where small hostile animals, such as the wolf and the wild boar, roamed; between Catalunya Square and the sea a lower lying plain, full of swamps with clouds of mosquitoes carrying deadly malaria, and surrounded by cane thickets; cutting through the plane in a gentle slope the rushing streams and "rieras" carrying spring and rainwater from the sierra to the sea; and bordering the plain, the two rivers, the Besós and the Llobregat whose deltas came together at the hillock of Taber and the mountain of Montjuïc on the coast. They gradually halted the alluvial deposits which would finally fill the plain upon which the ancient city of Barcelona was to be built up.

500 years before Christ the Iberian tribes known as the *Laietanos* settled in this privileged plain, protected from the worst north winds by the mountains and open to the sea for the arrival of the Phoenician and Greek traders. Laie was the name of their settlement, located on the summit and slopes of Mount Taber. The streets were very narrow with the square facing the sea and with small houses made of stone, in which families of peasants and craftsmen dwelt. The Romans chose this settlement to establish their small town, with the main square in the same place as the most famous square in modern day Barcelona, that of Sant Jaume (St. James). The name given to this town, Barcino, or Colonia Favenica Julia Augusta Paterna Barcino, to be more exact, has survived in its modified form. Thus, Barcelona was born, although some believe that the spirit of Barcelona was born long before when the Phoenicians and the Greeks instilled the arts of industry and trade into the hearts of the *Laietanos*. On the other hand, other people, such as the great scholar of the origins of Catalonia, Raimón d'Abadal, maintain that Barcelona owes its existence to the walls which enclosed the city in the fourteenth century to protect it from the Barbarian invasions, as it was only because of the walls that the city became consolidated instead of being wiped off the map and that it began to flourish again at the right time, well into the Middle Ages. These walls can still be seen today inside some buildings and also outside as they run parallel to the modern day Via Laietana, although they were renovated in the Romanesque and Gothic periods.

Trade, industry, and heavy Romanization soon made the primitive Barcino or Barcilo, into a city well integrated into the Mediterranean civilization and equipped for the practice of the art of navigation, in which it was later to excel. The city was still lacking in other characteristics to set it apart from others of the world. For the time being Barcilo was a subsidiary of the capital Tarraco.

The Northern Barbarians granted Barcelona a new privilege: in the fifth century Athaulf made it capital of his kingdoms in Gaul and Hispania, although only for a short time. The French king, Louis I the Pious or the Debonair, later conquered the city from the hands of the Muslims and made it into the capital of the most advanced county or shire of the Hispanic March. This county soon became independent of the Franks and began to form the nucleus for what was to be Catalonia in the ninth and tenth centuries. It thus added to its historical titles that of capital, the feature of progressive conqueror and the state of being a crucible for the birth of a new nation.

The Hispanic March, created by the Franks, was now rebuilt under the hegemony of Barcelona and was extended towards the south-west by its conquests. The birth of the Catalan language, derived from Latin, at this time was to be the consolidating factor. Barcelona grew and grew and occupied all the old Roman settlement, filling it with civil and religious buildings and also some private ones owned by nobles. It began to attract people from outside and a new impulse was thus given to the culture and economy of Barcelona. The Jews established themselves in the Call. Barcelona was able to compete with Genoa and Venice and was often superior to the former insofar as its power on the seas was concerned.

Luckily, many monuments of all these events have survived. It is difficult to find a more interesting pastime than walking through the "catacombs" under the old city, near the cathedral, which make up the achaeological area of the Museo de la Ciudad (City Museum), to see this long history at first hand, from the Neolithic age to the Middle Ages, with palpable specimens of pottery, bone, bronze, ivory, stone, house lined streets, funeral urns, arms, and works of art. One can then take a walk along the surface to see the old gothic palaces in the Plaça del Rei and then go on to the Cathedral with its religious relics, and many works of art. In the Plaça de Sant Jaume two palaces can be seen: that of the Town Hall and that of the Generalitat. All of the old quarter houses innumerable remains and interesting buildings which tell us of the glory and power of medieval Barcelona.

In that period of splendour Barcelona built new city walls to cope with the expanding city. The easternmost wall left the lower course of the "rambla" inside the city. "Rambla" is an Arabic word meaning "sandy bed" translated by "riera" in Catalan. The streams which flow into the sea are typical of the eastern region of the Iberian Peninsula. In Catalonia many of these streams or "rieras" have been converted into streets, often main ones, in view of the success enjoyed by the "riera" in Barcelona. In the fourteenth century the lower part of the Rambla was channelled so that the waters did not hinder walking and so the one-time stream carrying rainwater to the sea, which was at one time the eastern limit of the city, began to be a walkway and a meeting point for the whole city.

The period of decline began in the fifteenth century. Barcelona, and all Catalonia with her, had to begin to learn a lesson which still has not been fully assimilated because it is so hard. This lesson was having been important and suddenly becoming not so important; having once been a leading city, such as modern day Paris, London, New York or Tokyo and then finding itself nothing more than a provincial city. From this experience was born a certain feeling of victimization combined with the more positive one of wishing to recover the old power. People also learned to accept the brevity of human glories, to live with a sense of sceptical realism, as Salvador Espriu suggested, or to live the pleasures of life, as expressed in the poetry of Josep Maria de Sagarra.

During the long centuries of decline —as described above— the Catalans in general and the people of Barcelona in particular found the meaning of the saying "Every cloud has a silver lining". The depressed city began to put all its efforts into work and trade, and managed, by virtue of its wealth, to position itself among the most important cities of Spain at a time when these were in an even deeper state of decline after having yielded to the temptation of easy gold from the Americas and having been left behind by history.

This upsurge was as quick as it was fantastic. The old provincial city began to see itself surrounded by the utmost prestige. Its people worked so hard that work was almost a religion. They applied the traditional Catalan virtues of constancy and saving. Barcelona took examples from others and became modernized. It became a high-class, progressive city which believed in the powers of science, culture, and music.

And so these were the vices and virtues of the city as they had been pinpointed time after time by natives and strangers: hard work balanced by culture; individualism combined with corporate action; the love of money with a hint of romance; having one's roots in a small homeland made larger by universal curiosity; the tendency to shut oneself off from the pleasures of life.

As it is Now

Barcelona is at the same time both a modern and an ancient city. The present day city has come down to us after many difficulties. The ancient city was built gradually through the centuries based on the Roman city with its two main streets crossing each other, the Cardo and the Decumanus, located in the present day Plaça Sant Jaume. The city was extended in the Middle Ages until its perimeter comprised the Rondas, the Plaça de Catalunya, Carrer Trafalgar, Carrer del Comerç, and, of course, the sea.

The modern city, however, grew very quickly –between 1880 and 1930 approximately– as it was then that the Eixample (expansion area), the project of the engineer Cerdà, was built. The old city was forbidden to expand outside its walls and therefore the upper plain was almost free of buildings, although small villages, such as Gracia or Sant Martí de Provençals, existed in the area. The expansion could therefore be carried out in a rational manner, with straight, uniform streets combined together in a far-reaching network to make up the largest expansion area in Europe.

The new city, however, has grown up between 1940 and the present. It could be described as an urban failure, with no order to its chaos, with no intelligent project to mediate between necessities and interests. The dictatorship would not allow the city to carry out any kind of planning. Chaos was the order of the day. Now the city and its administrators are determined to rearrange and rebuild all these suburban areas so that they may take their place alongside the two cities mentioned above –the old city and the modern city– and so that people may live a comfortable life in all the different areas. This is the plan for Barcelona at the moment and the possibility of the Olympic games being held in the city is regarded very optimistically. Such an event could give the city the necessary impetus to achieve this reorganization.

It is a well known fact Universal Exhibitions, important congresses and fairs, or the Olympic Games have often been occasions for important changes in the area of town planning, and Barcelona is well experienced in the subject. When the Universal Exhibition was held in the city in 1888, Barcelona changed from a provincial city to a cosmopolitan metropolis under the auspices of the mayor at the time, Rius i Taulet. The land left by the old military citadel was made into the beautiful garden of the Parc de la Ciutadella with many buildings designed in the new style which was later to make Barcelona so famous: the Modernist style. The economic aspect of the Exhibition was not particularly favourable to the city but as far as vigour, art, and town planning were concerned, the Exhibition was the making of Barcelona. The Eixample, which had got off to rather a slow start, began to take shape extremely quickly. Some seventy five architects, who either invented or followed the Modernist style, worked alongside numerous painters, glaziers, forgers, potters, and other craftsmen to put all the finishing touches to the buildings.

Several factors were involved in the splendid creation of the Eixample. Firstly, Barcelona had been restricted to within the city walls until 1850 and was desperate to gain more living space. It was only awaiting permission from the central Government and the military authorities in order to be able to expand over the plain. Between 1830 and 1850 the most progressive companies had converted their industries to steam and were working with a modern style workforce in medieval conditions. When the walls were pulled down, these industries were able to establish themselves in larger factories and increase their productivity on a large scale. Industry was at its height in the 1880's and there was talk of "gold fever", reflected in the famous novel by Narcís Oller "La febre d'Or". When the American and Philippine colonies were lost in 1898, large amounts of capital returned to the country and were of great importance in the expansion of Barcelona into the Eixample. Spanish neutrality in the First World War some years later brought great wealth to Catalonia, which could sell its products in Europe almost without competition.

The Eixample was a rational project, designed, according to its creator, Ildefonso Cerdà, to establish in the centre of Barcelona an equal society comprising contractors, traders, craftsmen, and workers. It was initially intended to be a Garden City and each block was to be built up only on two sides so that the generous central area could be used as a garden giving on to the road. It was never built for all social classes and nor was the garden project implemented as buildings were raised on all four sides of each block. Neither did the rationalist aspect triumph as the primitive simplicity of the project was annihilated by the ornamentation of the Modernist style.

The most positive aspect was the architectural one, with the triumph of modern aesthetics, and the great works of Gaudí –La Pedrera, Casa Batlló, the Sagrada Familia–, Domènech i Montaner –Casa Lleó and other important buildings–, Puig i Cadafalch –neogothic buildings intended to give their owners an air of antiquity, which, like the "nouveaux riches", they did not have–, and many other famous architects, such as Domènech i Estepà, Sagnier, Falqués, Rovira i Rabassa, etc. etc. Many such edifices are to found in the Passeig de Gracia, Rambla de Catalunya, Carrer Roger de Llúria, Carrer Pau Clarís, Carrer Girona and Carrer Bruch (especially where these meet Carrer Mallorca and Carrer València and it is here that the best of the Catalan Modernist style of those years of "vain madness" can be seen.

Although the social equality proposed by the progressive Cerdà never actually came about, the Eixample was split into two parts, with Rambla de Catalunya as the dividing line. The right-hand side (known as the "Dreta de l'Eixample") is mainly bourgeois and here the Modernist style is richer and more spectacular. The left-hand side (known as the "Esquerra de l'Eixample" in Catalan) was mainly occupied by the middle and lower classes. The many service buildings (the University, fire brigade, the Modelo Prison, the bullring, the Hospital Clínic, etc.) made this area into the modern popular quarter.

Towards 1930, when the Ensanche was practically finished, the traditional and also the new upper classes began to look for more open areas where they could have gardens. The conquest of the lands of western Barcelona began: the extension of the Diagonal, Pedralbes, and the higher areas, such as Sant Gervasi and Sarrià. As Cerdà's Garden City project had not been implemented, the Eixample had no garden areas to make the district pleasing to the eye and pleasant to live in. The right-hand side of the Ensanche began to be invaded by the offices of large companies and gradually came to be the main area of the city for the services sector.

The Universal Exhibition of 1929 also contributed to the reshaping of Barcelona. The main area affected by this was Montjuïc, the mountain located by the sea. Owing to its strategic position with respect to the ancient city, the mountain was also a military centre, crowned by the castle. In the twentieth century, however, it was no longer of interest as a point of defence and was recovered by the local corporation. The delights of this mountain had been discovered during the period of Romanticism and places of recreation and leisure, such as the "Gat" and "Trobada" fountains, were created where people went on outings on holidays. In 1908 the local corporation acquired a large area known as the Parque Laribal, where the famous del Bosque school, which was one of the most progressive in Europe as far as methodology was concerned, was in operation. The great reform was carried out, however, as has been mentioned previously, in 1929. Inspired by the projects of the architect Amargós, the authorities charged the Frenchman Forestier, one of the most important landscape gardeners in the world, with the creation of a great park with several different gardens. The architect Puig i Cadafalch (one of the great architects of the previous period –the Modernist period) directed the architectonic work. The implementation of the gardening work was entrusted to Nicolau Maria Rubió i Tudurí.

Several works were carried out in the immediate area where the Universal Exhibition was to be held: the Plaça d'Espanya was developed, several hotels were built (the work of Rubió i Tudurí), a large central fountain (the work of Pujol, who had been assistant to Gaudi) and also the towers at the entrance to the Exhibition itself (designed by Ramon Raventós). Inside the exhibition area itself was the Avinguda de la Reina Maria Cristina, flanked by enormous exhibition halls. At the end of this area are the steps leading up to the National Palace (now the Art Museum of Catalonia) with the luminous fountains of Carles Buhigas in the foreground. Among the most important buildings erected for this grand occasion was the Pabellón de Alemania (the Hall of Germany) designed by Mies van der Rohe, considered to be one of the most important works of the twentieth century. This building was pulled down when the Exhibition ended in accodance with the Exhibition rules. Plans have now been made to reconstruct this hall in the near future.

Other works executed for the Exhibition were: the roads leading to the area, the Greek Theatre, the Spanish Village (an architectural "collage" with reproductions of dwellings and general village atmosphere from all parts of Spain), and the great sports stadium. This whole magnificent complex is of particular interest to us now as the project for the Olympic Games facilities plans to use the mountain of Montjuïc and many of the installations already in existence as a nucleus.

Before we begin to speak of the reshaping process planned for the Olympic Games, let us take an overall look at the city of Barcelona.

First of all, let us look at the ancient city, which comprised three main blocks. The middle block –with its centre in the Plaça de Sant Jaume– is the oldest and houses the local government buildings (the Town Hall), the Autonomous Government buildings (the Generalitat) and also the Cathedral, several official buildings, churches and private edifices in old-style streets which make up the Gothic Quarter and immediate surroundings. On the right-hand side of this area, on the other side of Via Laietana, is the quarter of Santa Maria, with the church of Santa Maria del Mar and the aristocratic Carrer de Montcada (with its gothic, Renaissance, and baroque palaces, three of which have been bought by the Picasso Museum), and the Born (the old main market) and its promenade. It was in the higher part of this quarter where the textil industry began, which contributed so much to the economy of Barcelona in the nineteenth century. On the left-hand side of the Gothic Quarter, with the Rambla as the dividing line, the most popular, beautiful and famous place of the whole city to go for a stroll, is the Raval Quarter. This area is known for its wealth of medieval hospitals and also for its nightime entertainment of a popular nature. The quarter is also known as the Chinese Quarter.

Below the old part of Barcelona is the sea, which is of special interest for the future of the city. For many centuries now Barcelona has grown "with its back to the sea", in part because of the construction of the port, which closed off the open sea, in part because of the presence of the narrow gauge railway used by the port, in part because of the sports facilities erected on the Barceloneta side, and also in part because of the general neglect which characterizes the area between the Barceloneta and the area of Poble Nou. However, the Porta de la Pau (the Gate of Peace), at the end of the Rambla, the Passeig de Colon, the Passeig Nacional in the Barcelona, and the Passeig Marítim have been restored and have set the scene for the reshaping of the whole area.

Going uphill from the old city is, as has been mentioned already, the great central area of the Eixample. At present many of the beautiful Modernist style buildings are being restored so that they may recover their original splendour. A little further uphill from the Eixample is the old village of Gracia, with its popular atmosphere. At some distance are the quarters of Sarrià on the left-hand side, and Sant Andreu and Sant Martí de Provençals on the right-hand side. It is in these latter quarters that most damage has been done owing to the lack of planning, as has already been discussed, for the new, mainly working class, areas to be integrated into the city. The local corporation will have to make a special effort in these areas if a comfortable modern atmosphere is to be achieved. The large, bourgeois area at the end of the Diagonal, in Pedralbes, however, is well planned and has many gardens. Some easy, though expensive, improvements can be carried out in this area.

Looking towards tomorrow

As has already been discussed, the Universal Exhibition of 1888 led to the shaping of modern Barcelona –particularly where the Eixample and the Park of the Citadel are concerned–, and the International Exhibition held in 1929 was the occasion that stimulated the development of Montjuïc and its surrounding areas. Now, the Olympic Games provide an excellent impulse to remold the city, which has grown in such a chaotic manner in the suburbs, and to build in those areas which are at present undeveloped, such as the shoreline between the Barcelona and Poble Nou, part of the foothills of the Serra de Colserola, and also to extend the gardens of Montjuïc.

These projects are already underway and the Olympic Games, therefore, would just add more momentum. If the Olympic Games were not held in Barcelona, this redevelopment work would continue but at a slower rate. The preliminary plans for the reshaping of Barcelona include not only the central area but the whole of Greater Barcelona (the theoretical centrepoint of which is the peak of the Tibidabo mountain and a wide area of the Vallès), and also other, more distant places.

The foregoing pages have given an overall view of the economic potential of Catalonia and Barcelona and it has been shown that the country and its capital are well able to handle large-scale projects, especially now that autonomous political power has been recovered, which was not the case either in 1888 or in 1929. A summary has been drawn up of the sports facilities in the area and this has provided a good indication of the potential Barcelona and Catalonia have in this respect. We shall now go on to state more points concerned with this subject.

The enthusiasm of the Catalans for football is well known everywhere. This support is mainly due to the popularity of the Football Club Barcelona, which has one of the biggest stadiums in the world and many other facilities in the extension area of the Diagonal. We have also already mentioned the extraordinary importance of the Catalan excursionist centres but we should also point out that in this small country there are facilities and enthusiasts for almost all types of sport, as is shown by the existence of federations for many such activities.

To all the above we can add the excellent network of roads, airports, hotels, and shops. Barcelona also has many modern cinemas, theatres, dance halls, night clubs, and cabarets. Barcelona and the whole of Catalonia in general have a vast number of restaurants serving both traditional and international cuisine. To sum up we may say that the Catalan people are very open to foreign influence and that the country is in a excellent position, owing to the many tourists, to receive visitors from all parts.

For all the above reasons the preliminary plan for the Olympic Games begins with the statement "The programme can be carried out with ease", using the existing facilities and the various conditions mentioned in this article, which point out that a "concentrated solution must be chosen which will satisfy the Olympic requirements but which, at the same time, will allow the respective facilities to be spread over several strategically situated areas so that these installations can be used after the Games to cover the developments necessary in some areas. In a few words, the 1992 Olympic Games can easily be held in Barcelona and will at the same time contribute to the improvement and modernization of the city in general.

This short summary can only give an overall idea of the magnitude of the works to be carried out. This work can, of course, vary if more suitable options arise. It is quite clear that we are not dealing with Utopian programmes but instead with real and necessary programmes to create a solid platform of sporting facilities and to make Barcelona take decisive measures regarding the modernization of this cosmopolitan city in a cosmopolitan country. The traditional landscape should not be lost, either in the countryside or in the city; rather it should be restored intelligently and artistically.

Josep M.ª Carandell

INDEX OF PHOTOGRAPHS

1 Magnificent colours can be seen in this view of the Costa Brava from Tolosa to San Feliu de Guixols.

2 Volcanic "tranquility": Yaiza (Lanzarote).

3 The Basque Country, Alto de Ulcarregui (Vizcaya), offers the harmonious contrast of its traditional houses and the green symphony of its valleys.

4 The most famous image of Segovia, its Aqueduct, shows us how the elements can be harnessed to the benefit of Man.

5 Another "Museum" village of Spain is Santillana in the province of Santander.

6 Village full of light of whiteness from the work of the people: Casares in the province of Málaga.

7 An invitation to meditation in the cloisters of the Monastery of Guadalupe in the province of Cáceres.

8 The mysterious Alhambra steeped in legend....

9 Life in the Iberian Peninsula faces the sea: Port of Bermeo in the province of Vizcaya.

10 The watchtowers of los Cantones in the province of La Coruña seem to be designed to welcome the rain on their windowpanes.

11 Fishing is not just a sport; many Spanish families earn their living from it: Bayona, in the province of Vigo.

12 Traditional and original bathing huts on the beach at Gijón in the Asturias. The customs of an age gone by now provide us with a colourful image of the beach.

13 San Sebastián has such equilibrium and harmony that it is one of the most beautiful cities in Europe.

14 The Golden Tower and the Guadalquivir are still legendary.

15 The ultra-modern Calle de Alcalá is located in the gateway that opened the capital to the Mediterranean Levant and the statue of La Cibeles which identifies the city.

16 The harshness of the Pyrenees in Castillo de Loarre in the province of Huesca with all its natural beauty.

17 Salamanca, a city where every stone is an expression of history and culture, is the home of the oldest plateresque style University in Spain.

18 The Duchess of Alba scandalized her contemporaries when she posed for Goya like this: La Maja Desnuda (The Naked Beauty).

19 Picasso was born in Málaga but he studied in Barcelona. An attractive museum bears his name in the old part of the city.

20 On the edge of Catalonia and the Roussillon district, the medieval monastery of Sant Pere de Roda (Girona) symbolizes the magnitude of the old country of Catalonia.

21 James I of Catalonia, *the Conqueror*, during the battle for the conquest of Majorca.

22 The Valley of Bohí in the Lleida Pyrenees is at its most beautiful in autumn when the first snow appears on its rugged peaks.

23-24 The Greeks and the Romans left the mark of their period in Spain and they introduced the Iberians to the world of the theatre.
– Ampurias (Girona).
– Roman Theatre (Tarragona).

25 Many civilizations tried to conquer the country of Catalonia but it was able to defend itself from invaders. Tossa de Mar.

26 Perelada in the province of Girona, a refuge for people of good taste in the beautiful countryside of the Ampurdán.

27 If you want to listen to the nostalgic habaneras, visit the coastal resort of Calella de Palafrugell, the real home of this music.

28 The magic village of Cadaqués (Girona), the haunt of intellectuals and artists, is still authentic and not marked by the passage of time.

29 The Pyrenees provide those fond of sport with the magic of skiing, the risk of climbing and the beauty of the mountains.

30 The Ebro delta, a splendid ecological refuge and a paradise for migratory birds.

31 Peace, light and shade in the cloisters of Tarragona Cathedral.

32 Tortosa, in the province of Tarragona, reflected in the waters of the Ebro, with its cathedral in the centre of a sleepy city.

33 The harsh, spectacular rocks that protect the sanctuary of Montserrat and its queen, the "Moreneta".

34 The Cistercian monks settled among splendid vineyards and created the monastery of Poblet (Tarragona), which soon became one of the most important foundations of the Middle Ages.

35 The "castellers" keep up an old popular custom as they build their human castle in the Square of St. James in Barcelona. The feast of Our Lady of Mercy.

36 The Museum of Romanesque Art in Barcelona houses the ingenuous but evocative Christian frescoes of medieval art found in churches and hermitages in the Pyrenees.

37 Barcelona is a city where light, water, and art are beautifully combined. Its streets and squares are a spontaneous symphony of colour and unusual forms.

38 The busy port of Barcelona, which does not stop work even at night, seen from the mountain of Montjuïc.

39 The cable railway of Montjuïc allows one to contemplate the city, the quarter of la Barceloneta bordering on the sea and the beaches of this famous Catalan city itself.

40 The Woman with an Umbrella, a delicate and romantic symbol of Barcelona, in the Park of the Citadel, which can also be seen in the two previous photographs. The magnificent fountain is the work of the architect Fontseré, with the collaboration of Gaudí, who was very young at the time.

41 The narrow streets of the Gothic Quarter have maintained the traditional mystery of Mediterranean cities.

42 The "Casa de les Punxes" in the centre of modern Barcelona maintains the profound peace of its cloisters, church, and rooms.

43 The "La Pedrera" building, designed by Gaudí, is a permanent lesson in avant-garde sculpture.

44 The monastery of Pedralbes in sharp contrast to the dynamism and vitality of its surroundings.

45 The immense Park of Montjuïc has many sports facilities and also several important museums: the Archaeological Museum, the Ethnological Museum and the National Museum.

46 Columbus and the caravelle.

47 St. James's Square is the seat of the political power of the city: the Generalitat and the Town Hall.

48 One of the jewels of Barcelona, the Joan Miró Foundation, contains an important collection of this master's works. The Foundation building itself is one of the best works of the famous Catalan architect, Josep Lluis Sert.

49-50 The Picasso Museum is unique in its collection of works of the great painter, from his first oil painting – a portrait of his father – to the "suite" of "Las Meninas" by Velázquez.

51 The splendid Liceo Theatre is the largest of its kind in Spain. Opera has been performed there since the middle of last century and the best singers of the world have taken their bows on its stage.

52 Sardana lovers meet at the Cathedral door on Sundays.

53 The beautiful Cathedral of Barcelona is not only a place of worship; it is also visited by children and tourists.

54 The solemn basilica of St. Mary of the Sea, known as the sailors' Cathedral, embodies the elegance of the pure Catalan Gothic style.

55 The beautiful Plaza Real is the meeting place every Sunday for philatelists, coin collectors, etc.

56 The "magic" fountains of Montjuïc with the National Palace, now the Art Museum of Catalonia, in the background.

57 Barcelona celebrates the summer nights. The dazzling fireworks contrast with the classicism of the Christopher Columbus monument.

58 On spring and winter days popular races are held in the streets around the Montjuïc and Christopher Columbus monument area.

59 The wide roads of Montjuïc are often used for cycling races, motor racing and running, which attracts the people of Barcelona in their thousands.

60 A Barcelona man, Jordi Llopart, took his place on the Olympic podium in the 1980 Moscow Olympics.

61 When they are not involved in the tension of competition swimming, champions such as Isabel Mas like to relax in calmer waters.

62 The sports complex of the Real Club de Polo has one of the most prestigious showjumping circuits in Europe. In 1984 the best European teams have already tested their jockeys and horses for the Los Angeles

63 The Spanish Rowing School enjoys both high technical qualities and beautiful scenery in Lake Banyoles in the province of Girona.

64 The Mediterranean coast has always boasted many sloop owners. Some Olympic champions found ideal conditions for perfecting their techniques and training in Palamós in the province of Girona.

65 The artistic and pacifist beauty of Picasso's dove captured the attention in an almost reverent manner of the public who watched the 1982 World Cup. FC Barcelona.

Picasso
21.4.58.

20 21

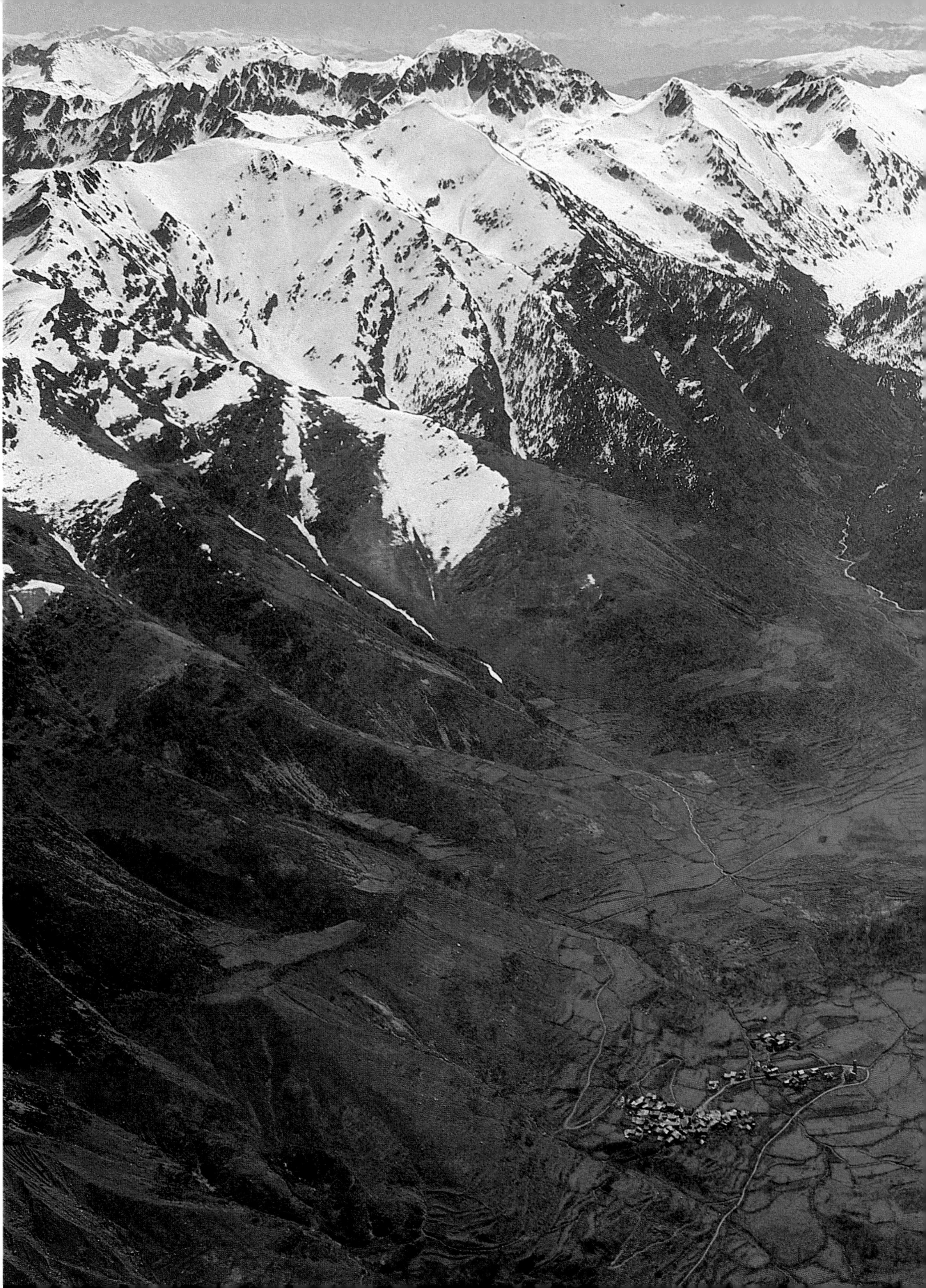

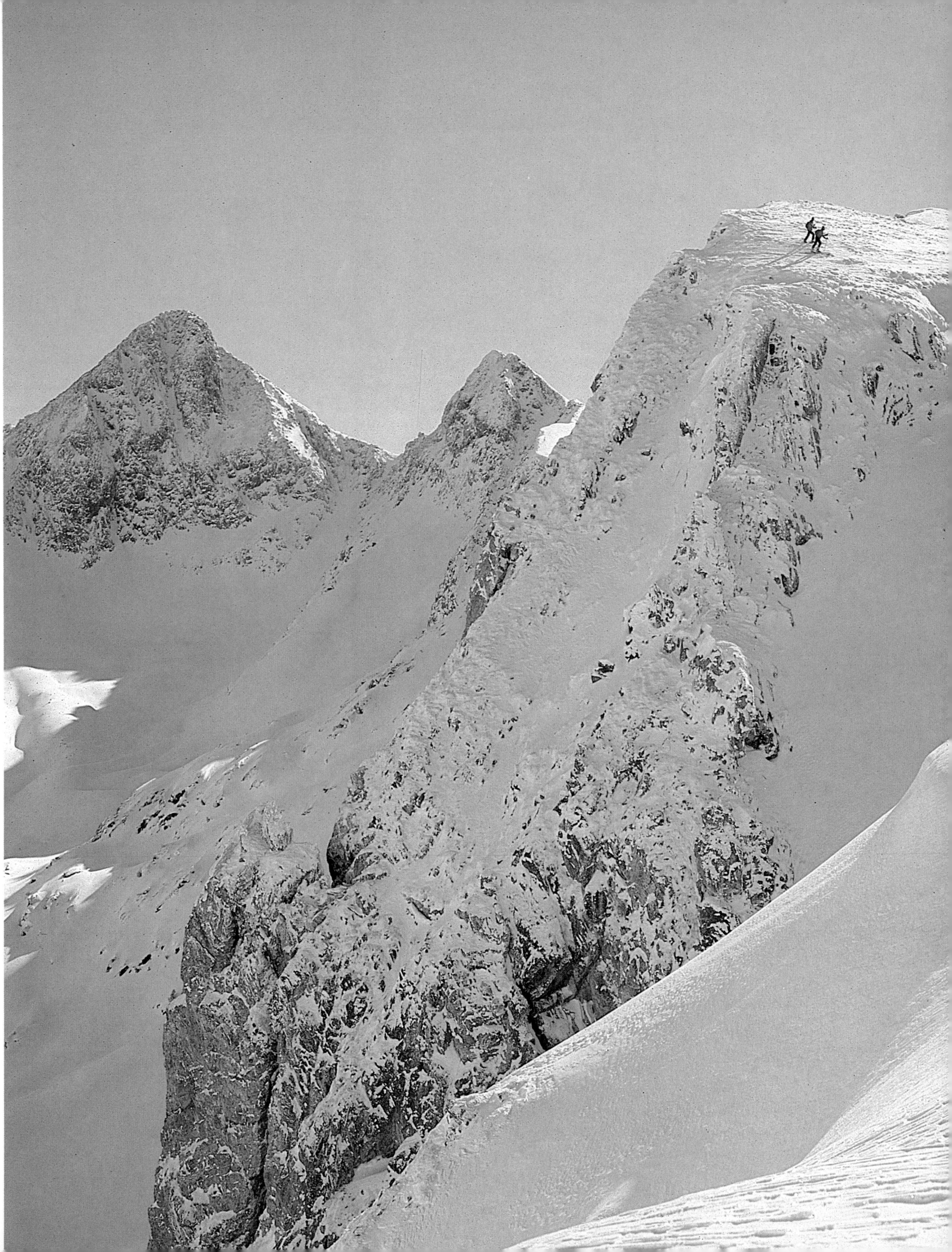

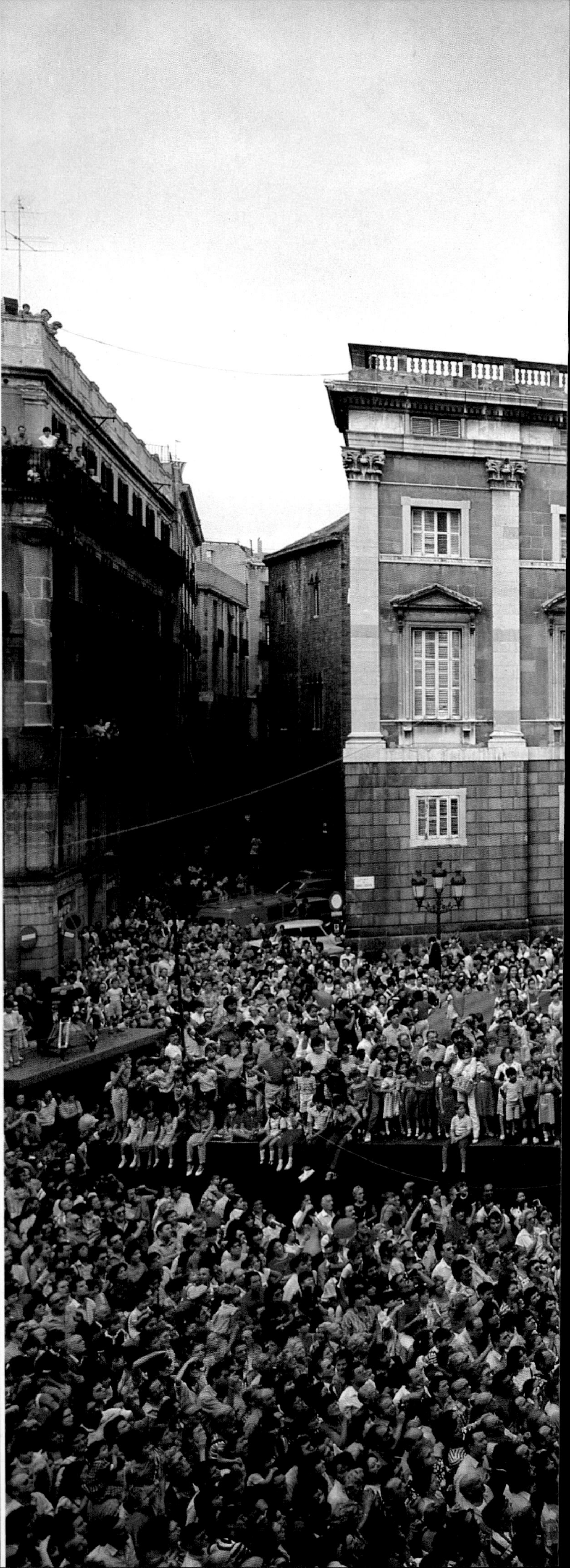

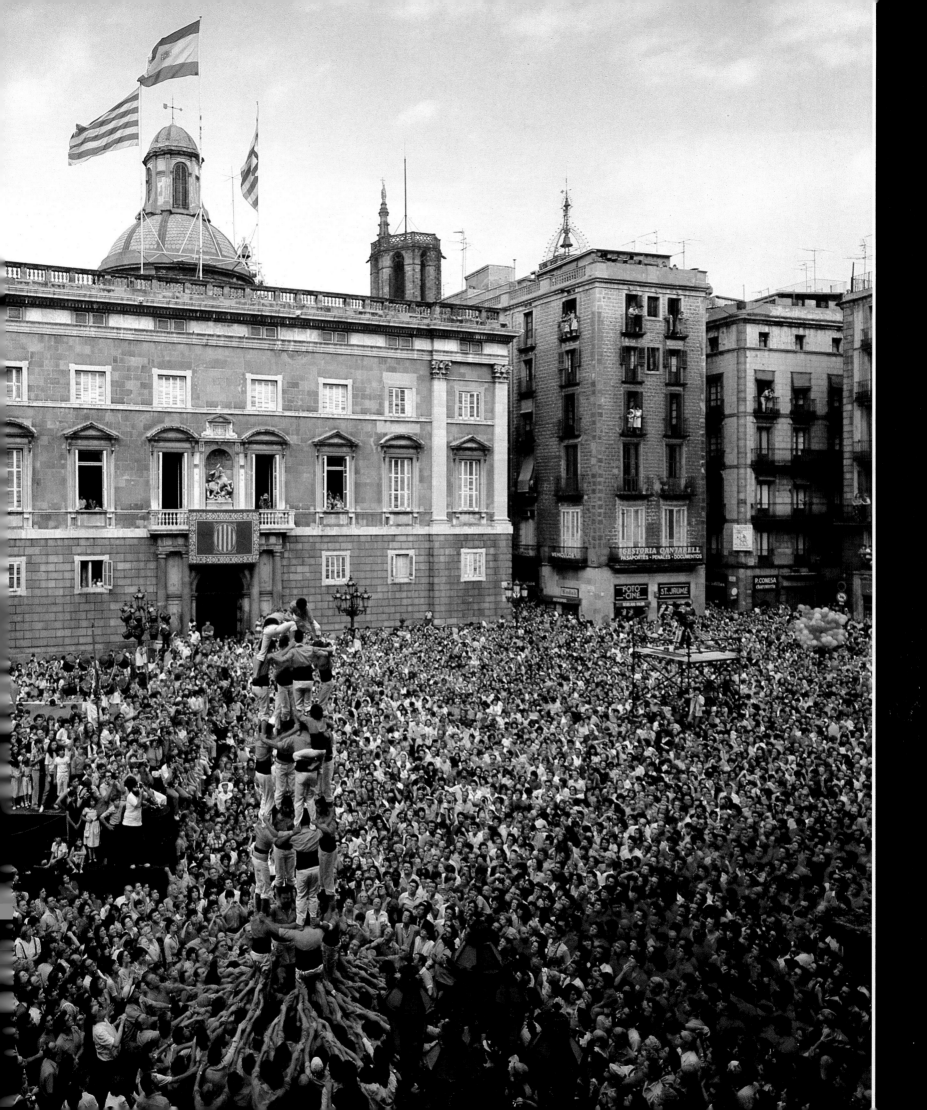

SUMMARY OF THE PRELIMINARY PROJECT OF THE CANDIDATURE OF BARCELONA FOR THE 1992 OLYMPIC GAMES

For the fourth time Barcelonaa is standing as candidate for the organization of the Olympic Games. Many different circumstances back up Barcelona's ambition to organize the Games and to reward five generations of faithfulness to the Olympic ideal.

— The rotation of the continents in designating host-cities for the Olympic Games.
— Spain has never organized any Olympic event.
— The fact that Barcelona and the surrounding area are well equipped for sports activities.
— The high technical level of Barcelona's managers and officials in the 23 sports which constitute Olympic events.
— The human quality the city wishes to impart in the 25th Olympic Games.
— The return to the Mediterranean and Hellenic concept.
— The universal character the Olympic Games always have and the fact thay they often coincide with the commemoration of an ecumenical event are in line with the coming anniversary of one of the most transcendental events of the history of mankind: the 500th anniversary of the discovery of America.

These objective data inspire great hopes for the acceptance of Barcelona as the host-city of the 1992 Olympic Games. There also exists a cultural essence and a special atmosphere difficult to express in words but which convey a serious wish to give sport a human quality that technology sometimes passes over.

The Hellenic tradition and even, perhaps, the Olympic tradition of Barcelona began in the 6th century BC when the Greeks founded the city of Empúries, where the first Gymnasium and Estadium in the peninsula were built. They were kept alive with the victory of the Barcelona man, Lucius Minicius Natali, in the 227th Olympic Games, which took place in 129 BC.

The Mediterranean world has always been the cradle and home of the Olympic spirit. It still takes man as the axis of society and this was the principle that inspired and made possible the Olympic Games, a refuge of the cult of man 27 centuries ago, the teaching of play, their cultural, pacifist, and fraternal aims, the Mediterranean spirit and the humanist tradition Barcelona and Spain have maintained.

The Cultural Olympics the Barcelona Olympic Games could achieve in the four years between 1988 and 1992 would bring out the ecumenical value in their concept but the cultural, artistic, spectacular aspects and the idea of work towards a common cause would be more evident than in any other edition of the Olympic Games in the past 25 years.

The 25th Olympic Games would be the culmination of a programme of popular education which would be implemented as soon as the Spanish candidature is accepted. This educational programme would reach primary schools, secondary schools and universities and would be particularly important in sports clubs, federations and other organizations all over Spain and a whole generation would be influenced by the pedagogical values involved in sport. The mass media, especially television, will be able to show the degree of maturity our experts, counsellors, and executives have reached.

The leading role the sports federations will play in developing the schedule of events for the 1992 Olympic Games will promote sport to our athletes and in particular to our children, the athletes and adults of the future, in the most efficacious way possible.

This will be the culmination of an educational programme that will find in sport and in the Olympic Games a valuable ally in the training of our young people and that will constitute a milestone in our contemporary history.

The project outlined in this report has been drawn up by the Olympic Office based on the guidelines given by the Steering Committee for the Candidature of Barcelona. The background, the reality, and the requirements for the future have all been taken into account as must be done if the candidature is to be presented in earnest. Experts have examined the sports, city-planning, administrative, architectural, technological, financial, social, pedagogical, and image requirements necessary for any city which seriously wishes to stand as candidate for the host-city for the Olympic Games with a minimum guarantee of success.

One of the most important points to be taken into account when seriously considering the organization of an event of the magnitude of the Olympic Games is the financial aspect. We have paid special attention to this point:

From the cost analysis made in the preliminary plan of the candidature of Barcelona for the Summer

1992 Olympic Games some data worthy of attention have been obtained. Although such data can serve only as a guideline, they are in line with the forecasts made and they have also been compared to data relating to previous Games.

The cost of organizing the Olympic Games is 42,640 million pesetas but net revenue from television rights alone could be 32,500 million pesetas. Although this latter figure seems rather high, it is in fact a very conservative estimate. These same rights for the 1984 Los Angeles Games will bring in 281,5 million dollars (43,351 million pesetas). The present forecasts are based on the Los Angeles Games, although it is expected that they will increase considerably for the Seoul Games.

The decisive participation of the *television rights* in the revenue earned from the organization of the Olympic Games means that Barcelona is able to present a balanced budget and feels it is well able to organize the 1992 Games. In view of this situation there will be stiff competition in future between many different cities in the world to act as hosts for the Games.

We have mentioned the figure of 42,000 million pesetas as the cost of organizing the Games. But how have we arrived at this figure? Have we simply extrapolated the costs of previous Games? In fact, the various organization points have been divided up into twelve headings. Each heading covers a group of subheadings under which the operations to be carried out are studied.

For each of the *subheadings* we have taken into account the staff necessary and the year in which they will have to begin work. We have also taken into account the financial cost of this workforce. For each subheading we have also studied the costs of goods and services the Organizing Committee will have to buy or hire, along with the necessary equipment. The total cost is the sum of all these points.

In the final balance for the Olympic Games part of the investment in equipment may be considered to be recoverable. Probable contributions from companies in the form of goods assigned may also be included. This will also represent a saving in the budget of the Organizing Committee. See the following table for the costs of each heading according to type.

Table 1

AREA	Staff	Services	Material	Invest.	SUM	Pos. Vol.	Total	Goods Assigned
		Expenditure						
1. Administration	1,735	2,500	775	725	5,815	0	5,815	300
2. Technology	416	2,929	3,882	8,671	15,898	0	15,898	1.300
3. Services	2,517	1,300	77	470	4,364	229	4,135	0
4. Press & Publications	898	0	1,084	0	1,982	0	1,982	0
5. Image	213	3,250	330	0	3,793	0	3,793	0
6. Build. Techn. Contr.	222	0	0	0	222	0	222	0
7. Security	638	624	135	113	1,510	0	1,510	0
8. Olympic Village	958	1,000	650	1,212	3,820	0	3,820	0
9. Sports	2,712	684	100	0	3,496	346	3,150	0
10. Ceremonies	254	658	124	0	1,036	0	1,036	0
11. Cultural activities	177	920	0	0	1,097	0	1,097	0
12. Youth Camps	91	25	30	40	186	0	186	0
TOTALS	10,831	13,970	7,187	11,231	43,219	575	42,644	1.600

SUM: Sum of the 4 preceding columns.
TOTAL: Net cost.

The *Sports Facilities* are an absolutely vital part of the final budget for the holding of the Games. Those who know the city of Barcelona and its surrounding area will think that sport is a part of everyday life and that, consequently, there are many sports facilities, both publicly and privately owned. Such an approximate view of the situation could be quite valid in the case of a different type of study but it must be seen in realistic light when dealing with a study for the organization of the Olympic Games. The results of the work carried out to assess the existing sports facilities surpassed all possible forecasts.

It transpires that in Barcelona there are a total of 78 installations which can be used for competition events, or training. Another 86 have been classified as *others* that could be used if necessary. The total figure includes the installations in existence at the present time which will continue to be in operation in 1992. If they are to serve our purpose perfectly, however, they will have to be improved (scoreboards, dressing rooms, flooring, etc.). 5,700 million pesetas have been reserved for this. Also included are those facilities which are being built now and those which are planned for in the investment budgets of the various public organizations for the coming years. Here 3,000 million pesetas have been reserved to bring these installations into optimal condition.

Finally, as far as sports facilities are concerned there are four significant actions to be carried out: the Olympic Pavilion, the Olympic Stadium, the Olympic Swimming Pools, and the Velodrome. These are obviously the most costly and the most involved facilities. Technically and architectonically they should fulfil the requirements of the modern world and a city like Barcelona in a country like Spain should have top quality sports facilities.

When the 1992 Olympic Games are held, these sports facilities should already be city sports facilities. It is the City Council's wish that the construction of these installations should be independent from the celebration of the Games. An example of this is the construction of the Velodrome, which will go into operation very shortly. Or the Olympic Pavilion, on the construction of which the Japanese architect Arata Isozaki has been working for months.

The overall budget for construction and improvements is 18,000 million pesetas, of which 60 % will be for the account of the Organizing Committee and the rest in form of contributions from public organizations. In drawing up these final figures the construction of a marina has not been taken into account as this will no doubt be an attractive project for private investment capital. The renovation of some of private installations taken into consideration and which work will certainly be done, the construction of the Sports Pavilion, the Velodrome, and the restoration of the Sant Jordi swimmming pool, will all be carried out between 1983 and 1986.

The *Press buildings*, both the main and auxiliary centres have been included under the heading of installations.

The Olympic Games are not the Games of one city, nor even the Games of one country. It is thought necessary for there to be an ancillary press centre in each of the basic event installations. There should also be a press centre in each different Olympic area covering a series of facilities. In this way the mass media can carry out their work effectively.

The most important ancillary press centre will be the one to be built in Montjuïc in the vicinity of the Olympic Ring. This area will comprise the Olympic Stadium, the Olympic Sports Pavilion and perhaps the Olympic Swimming Pool. As some concern was expressed regarding non-profitable investments, a study was carried out to see how this press centre could be used after the Games. It has now been decided to convert the building into a physical education institute or sports university.

It is planned to house the main press centre in the present Congress Hall of the Fair buildings. This building covers an area of around 30,000 m² and has good facilities. It is situated in a perfect position 500 metres from the Montjuïc Olympic Area, where the most important events will be held. There are excellent connections with the Catalan Railways, the airport, the Olympic Village and the other Olympic Areas. All these factors make the building ideal for the press centre. The total cost of the press centres and ancillary centres will be 1,500 million pesetas, of which 65 % will be for the account of the Organizing Committee.

The *Olympic Village* usually requires the largest investment of all but it will not be excessive in the case of Barcelona. Because of the situation of the Village and the facilities afforded by being Olympic outfitters, it should not be difficult to find private investors.

In the previous paragraphs the concept of areas has been referred to as meaning concentrations of sports facilities, which need, therefore, to be treated as city-planning projects. Although the areas mentioned below have been the object of careful consideration, they still have the provisional nature of a preliminary project. There will be *nine different areas* in which the Games will be held: Llobregat, Montjuïc, Parc de Mar, Diagonal, Vall d'Hebró, Rowing Canal, Marina, Badalona/Montgat, Vallès/Cerdanyola.

The conversion of the Llobregat area and its establishment as a city park would make citizens of Barcelona and those living in the industrial areas surrounding the city extremely happy as they would finally have a park which would provide some communities of Greater Barcelona with an outlet to the sea. The rowing canal and the archery ground could be built inside this park.

The Montjuïc area will be developed and made into gardens, thus completing the work begun in 1929 when then Universal Exhibition was held. This area has been an important breathing space for the people of Barcelona inside the city itself.

The Olympic Village is planned for the Parc de Mar area. This area will be in the Poble Nou quarter of the city. Communications are difficult, the railway prevents contact with the sea and the beaches are polluted. When the Bogatell purifier is brought into operation, the Montgat/Badalona drainage system connected, the capacity of the Sant Adrià drain doubled and the railway line buried under ground, along with other improvements to be made in the quarter, it will become an important residential and tourist centre.

The building of the Olympic Village in this area, following some of the guidelines set out by the brilliant Catalan city-planner, Ildefons Cerdà —open blocks, buildings with three or four storeys, adjacent sports and service facilities— will probably make this enterprise acceptable to private organizations and this is one of the reasons which has led to the study of the project.

The Diagonal area is probably the area with the greatest density of sports facilities —the Football Club Barcelona installations, Club de Polo, the University sports fields, the INEF, and the new l'Hospitalet facilities— but they have been built without any kind of city-planning. Some order will have to be brought to this area, therefore.

The Vall d'Hebró area will have the velodrome, two covered sports areas and a park.

The Banyoles area, a beautiful spot with excellent rowing conditions hard to match in this country and well known to experts in this sport all over the world, is one of the areas proposed for the rowing events. A small Olympic Village would be built and the existing facilities would be improved on.

The Marina, along with the rowing canal, is the only installation which has not been allocated a specific place. Any port along the Mediterranean coast would be acceptable although, whichever port is chosen, it will need some preparation, either for the residence of the athletes or in the town-planning aspect. Both the Palma de Mallorca City Council and the Balearic Islands Interisland General Council have offered to organize the sailing events for the 1992 Olympic Games.

The Badalona/Montgat area will complete the reshaping of the Barcelona seafront area and will have the same function for the north of Barcelona as the Llobregat area will have for the south.

Finally, the residential complex for the judges and referees for the Games will be built in the Vallès/Cerdanyola area. The building sector in this area is quite dynamic and it may be possible to get the private sector to take charge of this construction. For the moment, however, the idea is to build this complex inside or very near the campus of the Autonomous University of Bellaterra. After the Games complex can be used as a university hall of residence with sports facilities incorporated.

The total cost of the areas, including purchase of land, its development and preparation, will be 22,000 million pesetas for the period in question. The Organizing Committee would take charge of 50 % of these expenses.

If we add 10 % (7,500 million pesetas) for incidental expenses to the figures mentioned above, the Organizing Committee's *overall budget figure* is 73,250 million pesetas. The public administration quota for installations and work carried out would be 14,940 million pesetas, making a total of 88,190 million pesetas. But how will the Organizing Committee manage to raise the 73,000 million ptas. to which it has committed itself?

The *revenue earned by the Organizing Committee* alone is very important, equivalent to the total cost of the organization, which reach 42,500 million pesetas. The most important part of this figure, 32,500 million pesetas, corresponds to the television rights, which, as we have already mentioned, could be considerably higher.

The amounts corresponding to gate takings —2,450 million pesetas, accomodation in the Olympic Village— 1,200 million pesetas, programmes and posters —150 million pesetas, and services— 1,630 million pesetas, interest and other financial revenue —2,500 million pesetas— have been calculated by adapting to the Spanish economy the amounts spent in previous Games and also by means of the real costs of each of these headings. An extremely conservative estimate of the revenue from assignment of licences —2,000 million, and sponsors— 3,000 million —has been made. It was very tempting to use the Los Angeles-84 figures (revenue from these headings will be 20,000 million pesetas) but the difference in size between the Spanish and the United States economies made it advisable to treat these figures with caution.

Revenue from lottery has been estimated at 2,100 million pesetas. This amount could be earned by staging special lotteries instead of ordinary lotteries on two or three occasions during the Olympic period. A system similar to that used in the financing of the World Cup held in Spain in 1982 would ensure that the public treasury would not suffer as a result of these lotteries.

The football pools are directly derived from sport and the statutes of the Betting Foundation state that the profits derived from the pools shall be used to promote sport and sports facilities. 8,100 million pesetas have been provided for in the budget under this heading.

The issue of coins and stamps will bring in 4,000 million pesetas. The 5,600 million pesetas from the sale of shares correspond to less than 50 % of the value of the investments made in equipment (computers, television, furniture and fixtures for the Olympic Village and furniture and fittings for the offices of the Organizing Committee).

Finally, 8,000 million pesetas have been included under transfers from public administration from the increase in tax revenue generated by the holding of the Olympic Games. The budget summary table is the best illustration of the above mentioned points.

Table 2
ORGANIZING COMMITTEE INITIAL BUDGET
(In milliards of pesetas)
NOVEMBER 1983

REVENUE

I. *Organizing Comittee income*		42,43
I.1. Gate takings	2,45	
I.2. Accommodation in Olympic Village	1,20	
I.3. Programmes, posters and lithographs	0,15	
I.4. Assignment of licences	2,00	
I.5. TV Rights	32,50	
I.6. Services	1,63	
I.7. Interests & other revenue	2,50	
II. *Share in Revenue*		14,20
II.1. Lottery	2,10	
II.2. Football Pools	8,10	
II.3. Coins	3,00	
II.4. Stamps	1,00	
III. *Transfers & Subsidies*		11,00
III.1. From the private sector	3,00	
III.2. From the public sector	8,00	
IV. *Sale of Assets*		5,62
TOTAL		73,25
Pro memoria		
Equivalent value public administration direct investment share		14,94
OVERALL BUDGET FOR OLYMPIC GAMES		88,19

Table 2
ORGANIZING COMMITTEE INITIAL BUDGET
(In milliards of ptas.)
NOVEMBER 1983

EXPENDITURE

I. *Organization of Games*		42,64
I.1. Staff	10,26	
I.2. Purchase of property & services	21,15	
I.3. Equipping of facilities	11,23	
II. *Facilities (share quota)*		12,80
II.1. Sports (Competition)	7,92	
II.2. Sports (Training)	2,97	
II.3. Press - complementary	0,97	
II.4. Accomodation - complementary	0,94	
III. *Work done in Areas*		10,34
III.1. Basic costs	0,00	
III.2. Conditioning costs	10,34	
IV. *Incidental expenses*		7,47
TOTAL		73,25
Pro memoria		
Public administration share:		
Installations and actions in areas		14,94
OVERALL BUDGET FOR OLYMPIC GAMES		88,19

The financial analysis of previous Games assures us that both the costs and the revenue proposed in this preliminary project are quite in agreement with the results of previous Games. We are also sure that the financial effort our society will have to make for the staging of the Games will be well within its possibilities.

From the block diagram it can be seen that the financial effort made by Munich (31 per thousand) was quite considerable and that it increased drastically in the case of Montreal (56 per thousand), mainly owing to technical problems. The small amount stated for Los Angeles (2,6 per thousand) is because of its large population and also because of the large number of facilities which already exist. In the case of Barcelona the figure would be 16,7 per thousand. This is quite a balanced figure, obviously higher than that of Los Angeles but lower than that for Munich and lower by far than the Montreal figure. In making the calculations for this financial effort it was taken that all the overall budget for each Olympic Games came from funds generated inside the country. In fact, in the case of Barcelona around 50 per cent of revenue will come from outside and the financial effort required from Barcelona, therefore, will be around 6 per thousand.

In the *analysis of revenue* of the various editions (Diagrama B) of the Games a constant evolution in the distribution of entries can be seen. While in the case of Munich the issue of coins was the most important contribution to the budget, this is not even present in the forecasts for Los Angeles and is shown as only a very small amount for Barcelona. Lottery, which was at its most intense in Moscow —Olympic lottery was sold in all the countries of the Eastern Block— disappears again in the Los Angeles figures to appear again, together with football pools, in an important position in the Barcelona Games.

The sum of the revenue from television rights, gate takings, athletes' fees, assignment of licences, and sponsors is 106 % in Los Angeles (mainly because of television and sponsors). These amounts are much lower in previous Games and the figure is 69 % in the case of Barcelona.

To sum up, the evolution of the distribution of revenue by percentages depends, of course, on the idiosyncrasies of each host country and also on its socio-economic features. It also depends on the television rights, however. While the television rights in the Munich 1972 Games amounted to 1 % of revenue, and 1.4 % in Montreal 1976, they increased to 35 % in the case of Los Angeles 1984 and 36.8 % for Barcelona 1992. As has been already mentioned above, once the Seoul negotiations have finished, this figure may be able to be increased.

The staging of the Olympic Games in Barcelona in 1992 is a desirable project from all points of view. It will give Barcelona, Catalonia, and Spain a good image and will heighten their international prestige. Such a project will give drive to the economy and will act as a catalyst for investments. Most of all, however, it will provide our society with a common aim. It will channel the hopes of young people and people in general towards one goal and will motivate them in the present situation of lack of incentive.

The possibility of Spain's becoming again, after 500 years, the capital of the world leaning on three main axes, the economic and commercial, the Universal Exhibition in Seville, the political, Madrid, and the sporting importance of Barcelona 1992 give the project even more incentive. The King of Spain presiding over the opening ceremony of the Olympic Games and proclaiming the event to the world is an act of such consequence that it goes beyond the possibilities of this book.

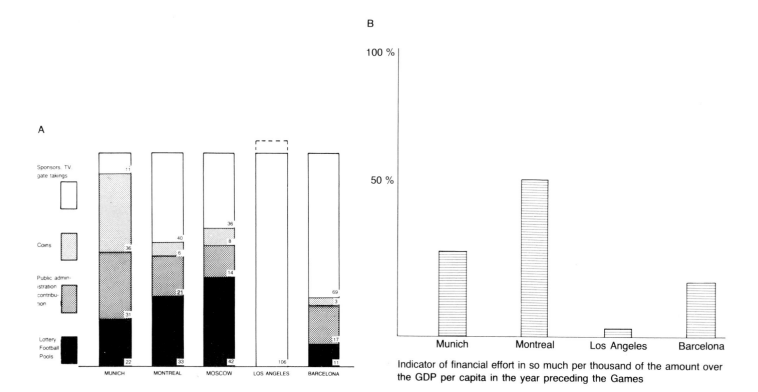

Indicator of financial effort in so much per thousand of the amount over the GDP per capita in the year preceding the Games

OLIMPIC GAMES 1992
AREAS

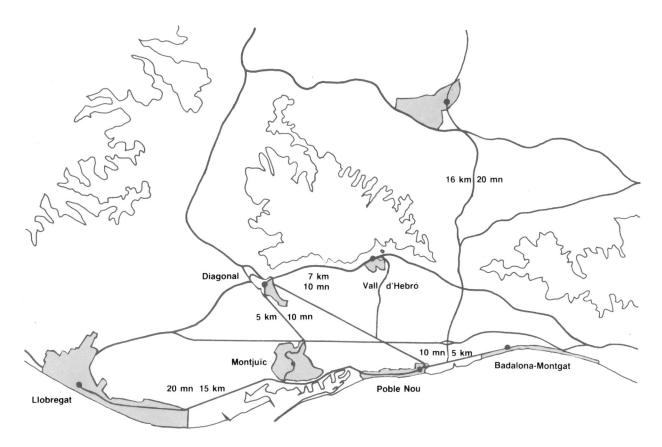

In the image, the following labels appear: Diagonal, 7 km 10 mn, Vall d'Hebró, 16 km 20 mn, 5 km 10 mn, Montjuïc, 10 mn 5 km, Badalona-Montgat, 20 mn 15 km, Poble Nou, Llobregat

Outline and general criteria

The sports facilities for the 1992 summer Olympics will be grouped together in various parts of the city in so called Olympic areas. The criteria for concentrating the facilities in different areas are as follows:

To optimize accessibility during the course of the Games, by concentrating a good number of the facilities in four central areas –Montjuïc, Diagonal, Parc de Mar, and Valle Hebrón–, which are well communicated among themselves and also with the Olympic Village. None of these areas is more than 5 kilometres from another and the journey would not take more than twenty minutes using either public or private means of transport. Thus we would not have a very concentrated set of facilities which could cause serious congestion, but neither would the facilities be so spread out that the spectacle of the Games would be weakened and the movement of both participants and spectators would be made difficult.

Three other peripheral areas are arranged around these four central points: the Park of the Llobregat, to the west; Badalona-Montgat, to the east; and Vallés-Cerdanyola, to the north. These areas have good connections with the centre and the Olympic Village by motorways and urban dual carriageways. The distance from these peripheral areas to Montjuïc or Parc de Mar is not more than 12 kilometres and travelling time is about half an hour using either public or private transport. In addition to being connected to the city by motorways, these peripheral areas are also served by the railway and underground railway network.

Situate the facilities in a suitable position with respect to the structure of the city, by locating the facilities nuclei in the best possible place to reinforce the idea of completion of the city. Four areas are located along the shoreline –the Park of the Llobregat, Montjuïc, Parc de Mar, and Badalona-Montgat–, the idea being that they should coincide with the end of the sea area of the Metropolitan Corporation of Barcelona. At the present time this area, comprising 42 kilometres of coastline and 28 kilometres of beaches, is underexploited, badly communicated, and severely polluted. The equipment proposal is linked to an important number of measures to be taken, such as the care and protection of the beaches, the channelling of the River Llobregat, completion of the road network and other means of approach, recovery and conservation of complexes of ecological importance, the development of the coastal parks, the urban

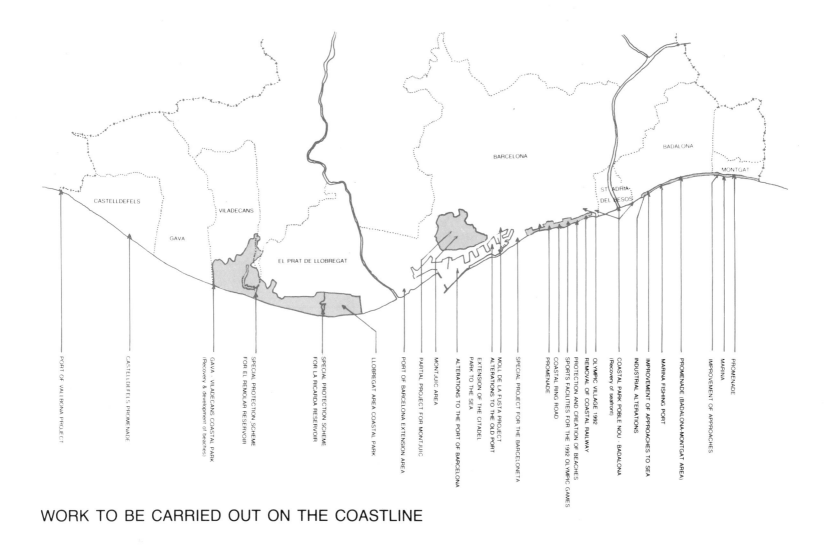

PORT OF VALLBONA PROJECT · CASTELLDEFELS PROMENADE · GAVA - VILADECANS COASTAL PARK (Recovery & development of beaches) · SPECIAL PROTECTION SCHEME FOR EL REMOLAR RESERVOIR · SPECIAL PROTECTION SCHEME FOR LA RICARDA RESERVOIR · LLOBREGAT AREA COASTAL PARK · PORT OF BARCELONA EXTENSION AREA · PARTIAL PROJECT FOR MONTJUIC · MONTJUIC AREA · ALTERATIONS TO THE PORT OF BARCELONA · PARK TO THE SEA · EXTENSION OF THE CITADEL · MOLL DE LA FUSTA PROJECT ALTERATIONS TO THE OLD PORT · SPECIAL PROJECT FOR THE BARCELONETA · COASTAL RING ROAD PROMENADE · SPORTS FACILITIES FOR THE 1992 OLYMPIC GAMES · PROTECTION AND CREATION OF BEACHES · REMOVAL OF COASTAL RAILWAY · OLYMPIC VILLAGE 1992 · COASTAL PARK POBLE NOU - BADALONA (Recovery of seafront) · INDUSTRIAL ALTERATIONS · IMPROVEMENT OF APPROACHES TO SEA · MARINA FISHING PORT · PROMENADE (BADALONA-MONTGAT AREA) · IMPROVEMENT OF APPROACHES · PROMENADE · MARINA · IMPROVEMENT OF APPROACHES

WORK TO BE CARRIED OUT ON THE COASTLINE

restoration of the various areas giving on to the sea, the restoration of residential complexes in bad condition, the reconversion of disused industrial areas, and the planning and development of a promenade along the shoreline.

Two other areas –Diagonal and Valle de Hebrón– will carry out a similar mission regarding the mountain line of Barcelona and will provide two means of access to the great park of Collcerola. The idea is to also form a "mountain front" with the actions to be carried out on the road network, parks and facilities.

Locate the sports facilities in line with a re-equipment programme. The four central Olympic areas Montjuïc, Diagonal, Valle de Hebrón and Parc de Mar fundamentally fulfil an urban mission: to be equipment centres on an urban level with services extending to the districts in the immediate surroundings. This network of district facilities will be located ring fashion around Barcelona and will contain the facilities we could refer to as "heavy", which need to be exploited to a high degree if they are to be profitable; the easy communications and their equidistant location have the result that an important section of the population is within the "catchment area" of each complex. Also, the size of these complexes would make it impossible to locate them in more central areas. This higher link in the hierarchy of facilities of the sports system will be completed by means of a suitable facilities plan, with other installations of a smaller type (quarter or district) for immediate use by residents or schools.

To adopt a metropolitan concept of the re-equipment process applying the same criteria for the remaining part of the Corporation. The area of the Llobregat will have a fully equipped park. This area will serve the population of El Prat, St. Boi, Viladecans, Gavà, and Castelldedefels, and also to some degree

Hospitalet and Cornellà. Similarly, the Badalona-Montgat area will comprise a fully equipped promenade along the seafront which will serve St. Adrià, Sta. Coloma, Badalona, Montgat, and Tiana.

The above plans are completed with the Llobregat axis, where various training facilities will be housed and which will serve the populations of St. Boi, St. Vicenç dels Horts, Molins de Rei, Pallejà, Papiol, St. Joan Despí, St. Just Desvern, Esplugues, and Cornellà.

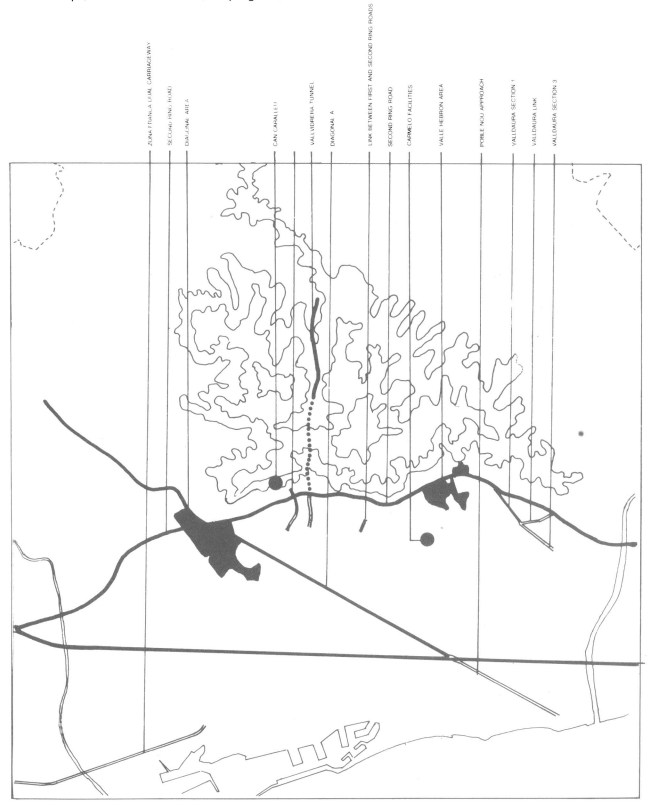

WORK PLANNED FOR THE AREAS LOOKING ONTO THE MOUNTAIN

A series of installations in the Besós-Ripollet axis will also be considered, with a more important focal point in the Cerdanyola area and linked to the Autonomous University. The towns of Montcada, Ripollet, Cerdanyola, and Barberà del Vallés will revolve around this axis.

Special consideration should be given to the large towns very near Barcelona: Terrassa, Sabadell, Granollers, and Mataró. These towns have a long sporting tradition and a high degree of organizational skill and are thus proposed for the holding of some of the Olympic events. The location of facilities in these cases will call for a detailed study of the urban conditions of each town.

The Montjuïc Area

Montjuïc will doubtlessly be the most important complex of all the different sets of facilities where the 1992 Olympic Games are planned to be held. The reasons for awarding such an important role to Montjuïc are twofold: its excellent sporting facilities and its symbolic nature.

Montjuïc is located in an extremely favourable, very central position and is well communicated. It is near the port and is surrounded by important roads, such as the Cinturón Litoral (coastal ringroad), Gran Via, Passeig de la Zona Franca, and the Paral·lel. It is easy to travel from here to Poble Nou, which is where the Olympic Village will probably be situated and which is located at 11.5 kilometres, 15 minutes by car. The airport is 9.5 kilometres away. Montjuïc is very near Sants station, one of the two main stations of Barcelona, which has links with the entire rail network. There is an Underground station in the Plaça d'Espanya at the entrance to Montjuïc itself.

Montjuïc is representative of Barcelona, both by virtue of its beautiful landscapes –a landmark for Barcelona and also a balcony over the city– and because of its sheer magnitude. The area is the largest park in the city and is also very important because of the many sports and cultural events which have been held there since its creation in 1929 for the International Exhibition.

The whole developed area of the mountain has become the most used space in the city for leisure activities.

As far as public sports facilities are concerned Montjuïc has more such installations than anywhere else in the city of Barcelona. The proposal is to use the present facilities but to remodel the Olympic stadium thoroughly and to build a new sports pavilion (this is already underway).

The following competition and training facilities are planned for this area: Olympic Stadium; 20 km walking circuit; 3. 50 km walking circuit; Serrahima Stadium; Julià de Capmany Stadium; La Fuixarda Stadium; Serrahima Stadium for shop put, discus throwing, etc.; Olympic Hall; Municipal Sports Pavilion; Pau Negre Stadium; Bernardo Picornell Swimming Pools; Palau Nacional; Ancillary Press Centre and future Physical Education Centre; Press Centre; Montjuïc Swimming Club (athetics and swimming); Palace of Alfonso XIII; La Fuixarda Gymnasium; Olympic Pavilion Training Areas; Victoria Eugenia Palace; Metallurgy Hall; Hall number 1; and shooting range.

The most important Olympic events will be held in the above mentioned areas: Athletics, Gymnastics, Waterpolo, Table Tennis, some Hockey, and the finals of Basketball, Handball, Volleyball, and Boxing. Many warming up and training facilities along with other auxiliary installations will complete the Montjuïc complex.

Olympic Ring. One of the axes in the organization of the 1929 International Exhibition, the one which departed from the Stadium and ran in a south westerly direction, will be the backbone of the Montjuïc Olympic Area. As the centre point of this axis, the remodelled Stadium will be the representative piece of the 1992 Barcelona Olympiad and will comprise the centre of the "Olympic Ring".

In August 1983 eight teams of very prestigious architects: Vittorio Gregotti (Italy), Arata Isozaki (Japan), Francisco Sáenz de Oiza and Rafael Moneo (Spain), José Antonio Coderch (Spain), Federico Correa and Alfonso Milà (Spain), and Ricardo Bofill (Spain) were invited to express their ideas for the Olympic Ring of Montjuïc so that some buildings could be designed and others remodelled to integrate them in an arrangement with a square leading into the precinct, and an avenue and reception area.

In January 1984, the Governing Council for the Barcelona Candidature, having examined the projects

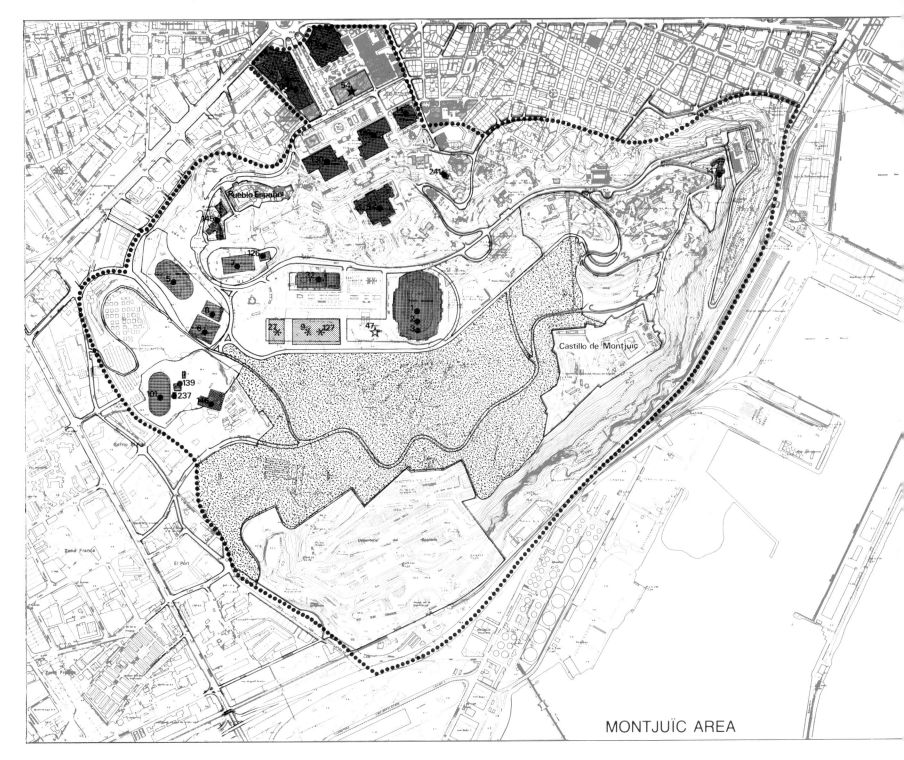

MONTJUÏC AREA

presented, decided to take as the basis of the design of the complex the project presented by Federico Correa, Alfonso Milà, Joan Margarit, and Carles Buxadé, as this project was, according to a statement made by the Mayor of Barcelona, Pasqual Maragall, during a press conference held to present the results of the tender, "that which best represented the civic character of Montjuïc as a park and that which best interrelated its function as a green area with its sports objective. Also chosen were Arata Isozaki's project for the sports pavilion, Ricardo Bofill's for the press centre, and Vittorio Gregotti's for the remodelling of the Olympic Stadium in collaboration with the other teams. It was also decided to appoint Weidle as technical sports advisor.

The final project drawn up by the above mentioned architects will be presented along with the Barcelona Candidature to the International Olympic Committee. The project for the Olympic Sports Pavilion awarded to the Japanese architect Isozaki, is now very advanced and the building will be opened in 1986/87. The projects for the other buildings are also underway: the Physical Education Centre

(Ancillary Press Centre), the remodelling of the Olympic Stadium, the restoration of the Bernardo Picornell Swimming Pools and the transfer of the new Pau Negre Hockey Stadium.

The framework of these projects is contained in the Special Project for the Mountain of Montjuïc. The preliminary project has already been approved and the project itself is now being drawn up. When this project has been approved, the projects for the planning of the road network on the mountain will be drawn up along with projects designed to improve the approaches. Finally, the Migdia Park project is to be drawn up, thus completing the planning landscaping of the whole Montjuïc area.

The Diagonal Area

This area is located at the W exit of the A-2 Motorway into Barcelona and will cover 120 hectares. This area will take up most of the space inside the shape formed by: Avinguda Diagonal, the First Ring road, Travessera de les Corts, Carretera de Sants-Creu Alta and the Second Ring Road (under construction). Two lines of the Underground serve the area and a large number of city buses run along the above mentioned roads. The area may therefore be considered easily accessible within the city.

The Diagonal area is one of the most recent city developments. The work has been carried out well and the area has many facilities and interesting features, such as the Pedralbes Palace, the University area, and the Cervantes Park. The most modern and luxurious hotels in the city are also to be found in this area.

The Diagonal area is second only to Montjuïc in the number of sports facilities, the difference being that, while most of these facilities are public property in Montjuïc, in the Diagonal they are almost all privately owned, or on a community basis. The Football Club Barcelona and the Real Club de Polo own half of the area and most of the facilities belong to these entities. Many of the remaining installations are in the University grounds.

We thus have a large area with all types of facilities, most of which are top quality and have high seating capacities. These facilities are ready for immediate use as training and event areas.

It is planned to use the following facilities for training and actual events: the "Blaugrana-1" sports pavilion of the Football Club Barcelona (FCB); The FCB Ice Rink; the FCB Camp Nou Stadium; The Real Club Deportivo Español of Barcelona football stadium; the FCB Miniestadi stadium; the Hospitalet Football Club ground; Real Club de Polo (equestrian events); Horse racing; Hospitalet Sports Pavilion; Pentathlon (long-distance circuit); Barcelona Tennis Club; Real Club de Polo (tennis); Turó Tennis Club; Archery; Ancillary Press Centre; FCB Athletics Tracks; Hospitalet Athletics Tracks (at project stage); the "Blaugrana-2" sports pavilion of the FCB; The Institut Nacional de Educació Fisica (INEF) in Esplugues; The Barcelona Squash Courts; the University campus sports pavilion; the Hospitalet sports pavilion (at project stage); the La Masía football ground of the FCB; Horse riding circuit; Real Club de Polo (hockey).

The following events will be held in the Diagonal Area: Basketball, Fencing, Football, Equestrian events, Judo, Pentathlon, Tennis, and Archery.

Although the Diagonal Area has sizeable facilities, there is no special project as yet for access to the area, parking, arrangement of the facilities, etc. It will be necessary, therefore, to draft a Special Plan, and in fact the preliminary work began on this project six months ago. This plan will affect the local corporations of Barcelona, Esplugues, Hospitalet, and Sant Just. This plan will also deal with the present facilities available and access to park and facilities areas which have not yet been erected but which are mentioned in the Metropolitan General Plan.

The Parc de Mar

Barcelona's contact with the sea is not as comprehensive as one would imagine and indeed wish. The Poble Nou area is located along the shoreline and is a popular quarter of Barcelona. It has a very strong "personality" as it is rather isolated from other areas of the city. It began to grow in leaps and

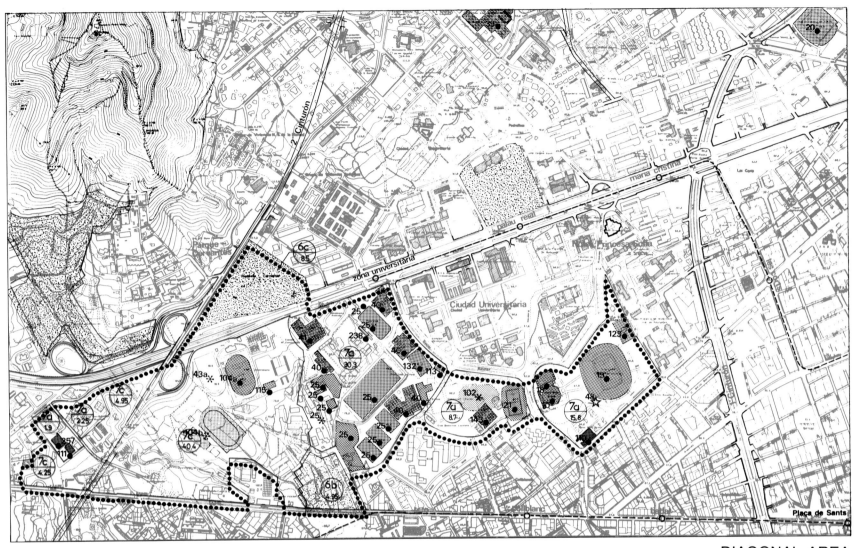

DIAGONAL AREA

bounds at the turn of the century and became a residential and industrial area. Its urban structure is now complete and large scale alterations, which may be carried out in line with the coastal operation, are called for. The recovery of the Barcelona Llevant beach is at present underway. The area is being decontaminated by means of drainage channels and water purifying equipment. Other work is also being carried out to protect the environment using land recovered from the sea. This promenade will eventually be linked to the Barceloneta and will require another large-scale operation: the burying under ground of the railway which runs along the coast and the demolition of many of the heavier works connected with this railway. When this is done, an old dream of Barcelona will come true: the opening of the Park of the Citadel to the sea. If these conditions are fulfilled, Poble Nou will also give on to the sea.

The future Parc de Mar (Sea Park) will link the residential area of Poble Nou with the beach. The Olympic village could be an extension of this residential area, which would give a final form to the Promenade. It would also be the initial stage of an urban development process on an even larger scale. The sports, cultural, shopping, administrative, and leisure facilities will enhance the present projects.

The following training and competition facilities will be located in the Parc de Mar area: Fish Market; Parc de Mar swimming pool; Parc de Mar sports pavilion; Ancillary Press Centre; Olympic Village; Olympic Village athletics tracks and training facilities.

The events to be held in this area are: Swimming, the various Jumping events, wrestling, and Volleyball. The most important element in this area, however, will be the Olympic Village, which will be built along the promenade, opposite the present factory area. Here the aim is for the athletes to feel at home in the Olympic Village and to have surroundings conducive to success. The success of the athletes is, of

17

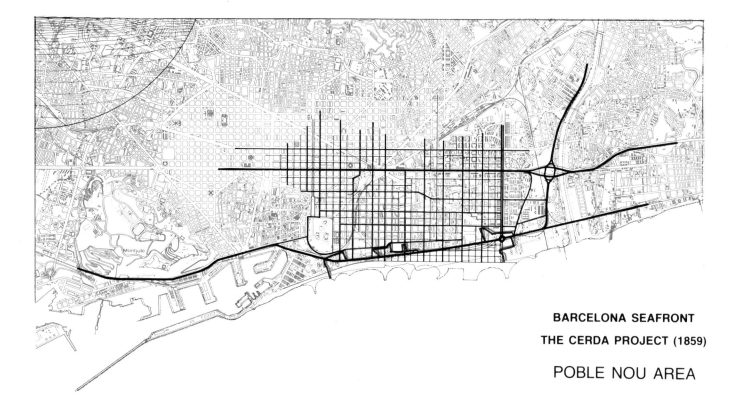

BARCELONA SEAFRONT

THE CERDA PROJECT (1859)

POBLE NOU AREA

course, the key to the success of the Games. Approximately 3000 people will be needed to staff the Olympic Village in the following areas: shopping centre, self-service restaurant, restaurants, leisure centre, games rooms, music, discothèques, sports club, theatre, post office, religious centres, car parks, sports facilities (swimming pool, athletics tracks, gymnasium, etc.). The success of Barcelona as the host city will depend on the ability of this small army of staff and on the functional aspect of the Olympic Village.

The Olympic village will have gardens, a bus station, and a shopping centre and will be protected by strict security measures. A radio station will broadcast in five languages to make the athletes feel at home. After the Games, the Olympic Village will be used to house the families affected by the redevelopment work to be carried out in Poble Nou. It will later be sold.

The work to be carried out in the Poble Nou area is the most complex of the whole Olympic Games project. Several additional studies to the General Project will be necessary, as will Internal Alteration projects. Studies to co-ordinate the various types of work have already begun and the Special Project for the Metropolitan Coastal Area is being drafted. Work is also being carried out on the project for the burying under ground of the railway.

The Valle de Hebrón Area

This area, located to the north of the Tres Turons, almost on the edge of the Sierra de Collcerola, covers some 40 hectares and is the largest undeveloped area inside the urban network of Barcelona. The Valle Hebrón area is strategically situated and this is the reason for completing this part of the city, by providing leisure facilities. The Barcelona velodrome has been built in this area. Near the velodrome are the Hogares Mundet with goods sports facilities which could be considered for training centres for the Olympic athletes.

The Parque del Valle Hebrón (Valle Hebrón Park) will be a large open area surrounded by sports facilities which will be used for the Olympic Games. The following facilities for training and events will be located in the Valle Hebrón area: the Barcelona Velodrome; the Valle Hebrón sports pavilion; Ancillary press centre; the Hogares Mundet sports hall; the facilities of the Unió Esportiva Horta; the Parque del Valle de Hebrón gymnasium; the Hogares Mundet swimming pool; the Guinardó facilities; the Hispano Francés facilities.

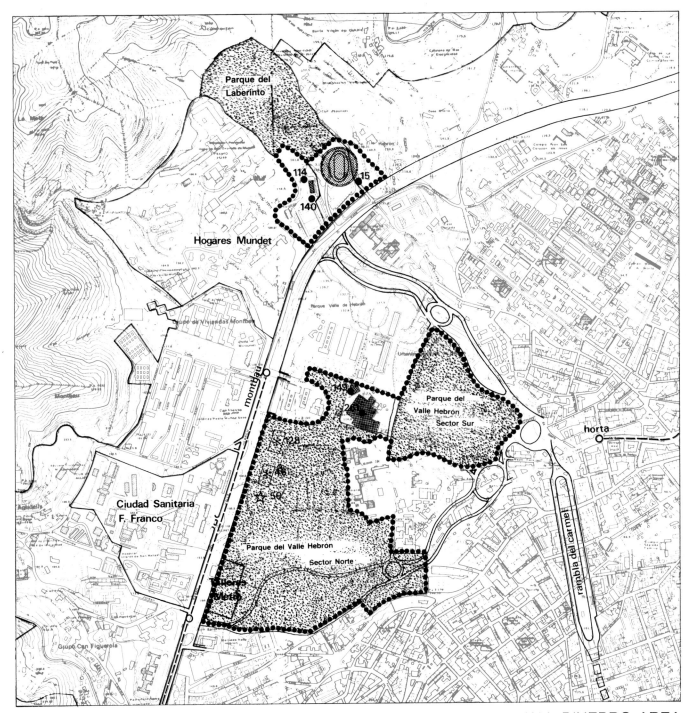

VALL D'HEBRO AREA

The Cycling and Volleyball events and the gymnastics training sessions will be held in this area.

The special planning and co-ordination projects for the work to be done in the mountain area are being carried out at present.

The Prat de Llobregat Area

This area comprises over 1000 hectares covering a distance of some 9 kilometres along the coast. The beaches are practically deserted. The fact that this area is located at the mouth of the Llobregat means that much of the land is marshy (la Murtra, la Ricarda, el Remolar) and is of great ecological interest as it is a stopping point for migratory birds.

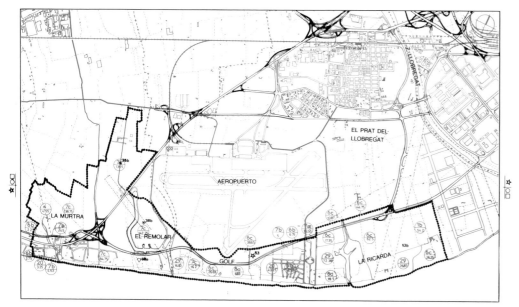

LLOBREGAT AREA

This area is sandwiched between the land surrounding the port of Barcelona to the east and the popular beaches in the extremely built-up regions to the west. Most of this land is on the coastline within the municipal boundaries of Prat but it is hardly used because of the bad communications, mainly because of the difficulties created by the proximity of the airport.

The present proposal of the creation of a great coastal park is in line with the wishes expressed at metropolitan level. The implementation of the park depends on improvements to be carried out in the communications area. An important road is planned to link the Castelldefels dual carriageway to the Zona Franca (and Coastal Ring Road) and to the town of Prat de Llobregat.

The necessary action will be taken to have the beaches in optimal conditions and it is proposed that the marshland should stay as it is, especially in the case of the main area, known as La Ricarda. The facilities of the Prat Golf Club are to be improved. The club is located in an extremely good position on the coast. An important sports complex would also be built to make the coastal park into an area to be used all the year round, particularly at weekends.

The training and event facilities initially proposed to be located in the Llobregat area are: Rowing Canal (alternative to Lake Banyoles; Archery ground (alternative to the Diagonal area); Ancillary Press Centre; Youth Camp; Pool for rowing training. All these event facilities are alternatives to other locations. Although detailed studies have not yet been carried out, it would appear that the area around the airport would be an ideal location for a shooting range complex. Facilities with the proper security measures could be installed here and the area is near the centre of Barcelona, with good communications.

The rowing canal, however, would involve extremely high construction and maintenance costs and the solution of using Lake Banyoles would appear to be more feasible. There would be no problem with the archery ground as this could be located by the Golf Club. The Youth Camp could be housed on one of the present camping sites if the present facilities were improved somewhat.

A special project concerning the mouth of the River Llobregat is being drafted and will form part of the co-ordination studies relating to actions to be carried out on the coastline. Under this project very important matters will be decided, such as whether to rechannel or divert the River Llobregat, whether to extend the port of Barcelona, the layout of the approaches by road and how to solve the problem of the bridges over the River Llobregat. These studies will be available during the course of 1984.

The Vallès-Cerdanyola Area

This area is situated on the axis formed by the River Besós and the River Ripoll, very near the Autonomous University of Barcelona. Communications to this area are extremely good as it is just off the B-29 motorway (Barcelona, Sabadell, Terrassa, and the future link to the coastal ring road) and the

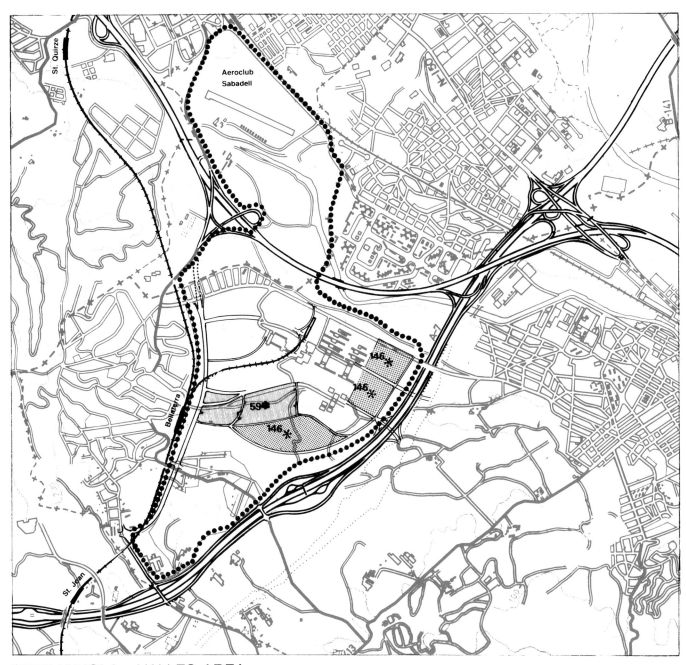

CERDANYOLA - VALLES AREA

B-30 motorway, Mollet-Papiol, the third ring road around Barcelona and the La Junquera-Girona-Tarragona (Mediterranean coast) or Lleida (inland, Cantabrian coast) by-pass. There are direct exits from both these motorways to this area and it is also served by the Ferrocarrils Catalans (Catalan Railways) on the Barcelona-Sabadell line.

The location of the Autonomous University of Barcelona in this area is in line with the old but current idea of the decentralization of Barcelona involving the establishment of activities and the erection of residential areas on the land behind the Serra de Collcerola, i.e. the Vallés. The setting of the Autonomous University of Barcelona is ideal as the geometric centre of an area with a population of around half a million over a radius of the 5 kilometres with the rectorate as the centre. The Autonomous University is planning to extend its campus, which is of great interest from the point of view of the Olympic Games.

The Special Project proposes the erection of a large residential area and sports complex in the vicinity of the University. Although there are no plans to use these facilities for actual Olympic events, as this would not be viable from the point of view of use of such facilities after the Games, they could be used as training areas as they are excellently equipped and well communicated. The residential area which is later to be used by university staff (both teaching and non-teaching) can be used to accomodate judges and referees for the Games.

As the Games will take place outside the academic year, other university facilities could be used for Olympic activities.

The Badalona-Montgat Area

This area lies along the coast and constitutes the eastern end of the metropolitan zone. It borders on the coastal district of the Maresme. There are about seven kilometres of beaches with pollution problems between this boundary and the River Besós, which marks the end of the Parc de Mar area. The population in the immediate coastal area is around 400,000. The beaches can be cleansed immediately as the final stages of work are being carried out to bring a drainage interception system into operation. This machinery would be positioned to travel parallel to the coast to avoid waste being emptied into the sea.

Several studies of the seafront are underway so that the above plans may be correctly implemented. These include some interesting proposals for the shoreline itself and the improvement of the approaches. One plan is to build a promenade to link up with that of Barcelona. This promenade would lead to various city, coastal, and leisure facilities. The promenade project will be supported by coastal protection work aimed at stabilizing the beaches and increasing their length and also, therefore, their capacity.

Along or near the promenade various sports facilities are planned, from very simple installations to indoor swimming pools. Finally, two marinas are planned which will be quite different from, but compatible with, each other. The Badalona marina is intended to serve the population in the surrounding area while the Montgat one, just off the motorway, will cover a wider section of the population of Barcelona itself.

The capacities for both marinas will be about the same, catering for between 600 and 800 boats each. They will help to palliate the lack of moorings in the Barcelona area for leisure boats.

Finally, two very interesting operations are planned for the outer limits of the area: to the east, the quarter of the Mallorquinas de Montgat will be completely altered and refurbished. This will generate new uses in contact with the port. To the west, there exists at present an area occupied by a disused factory, covering 30 hectares with 1,700 metres along the seafront. This area could be converted into a leisure centre and would give Badalona a new outlook on to the sea as well as linking up the promenade between the Barceloneta and Montgat.

The Banyoles Area

Lake Banyoles is a perfect natural setting for the flat water racing events. The size and location of this lake are described in full in the facilities chapter (   ). The attached map shows the town of Banyoles in relation to Girona, Figueras, La Bisbal, and Barcelona. It also shows how it is situated with respect to the airport and other approaches by road and rail. The possible locations of the Olympic village are shown, along with complementary facilities for rowing and other events.

The General Project for Banyoles is at the initial approval stage and no other planning is necessary at the moment. Projects will have to be drawn up, however, for improvements to the basic inland road network and approaches. The projects relating to the La Draga sports facilities area are already underway. All that is necessary for the preparation of the rowing facilities is to implement a cleansing and dredging process in a few areas. The location of the arrival platforms poses a few difficulties, however. A team of experts is studying the positioning of stands for the public and officials and also the press box. It is hoped that an economically viable solution with the necessary safety measures will be found.

BADALONA-MONGAT AREA

The Marina Area

This article does not deal with the location of the Olympic Marina. The study relating to the various possibilities is included under the Sailing Facilities section

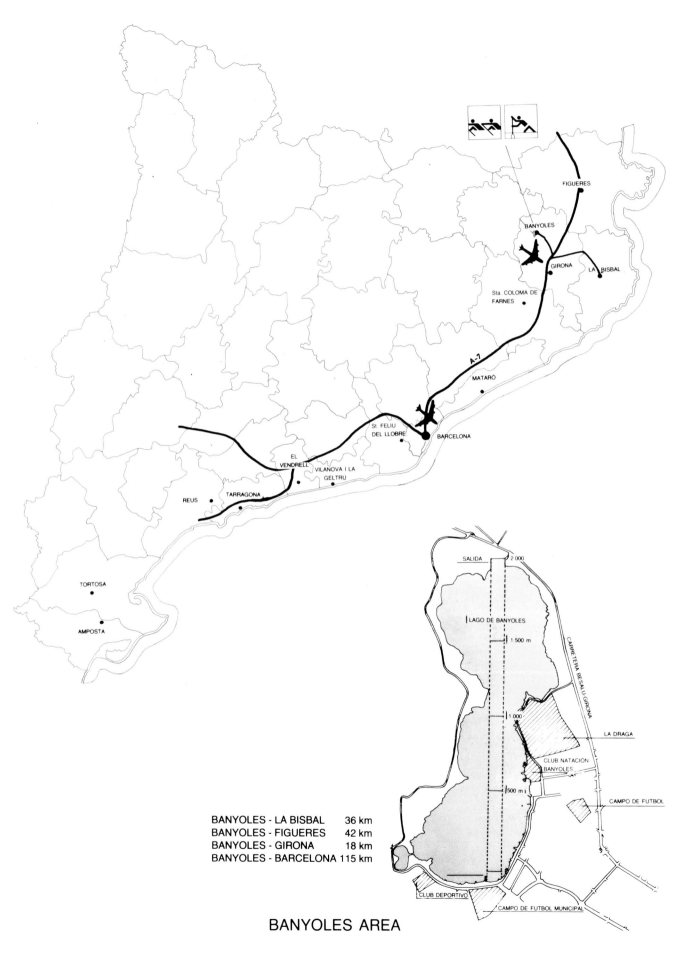

BANYOLES - LA BISBAL   36 km
BANYOLES - FIGUERES   42 km
BANYOLES - GIRONA   18 km
BANYOLES - BARCELONA 115 km

BANYOLES AREA

Cost of the Olympic Areas

Table (3) shows the provisions for the cost of the areas. The first colum shows the total surface of the area under consideration while the second column shows the surface area to be developed or made into gardens. The following three columns refer to the basic costs taken into consideration: purchase or expropriation of land, transfer of services and development of roadways. Beside the total costs for each heading is the cost per hectare calculated for each case. These are variable depending on the situation of each area. The next two columns list the costs of gardens and parks for the public areas. In these cases the cost per hectare is not applied to the whole surface area but only to that which is shown in brackets in the same box. The last column states the total costs in millions of pesetas (1983).

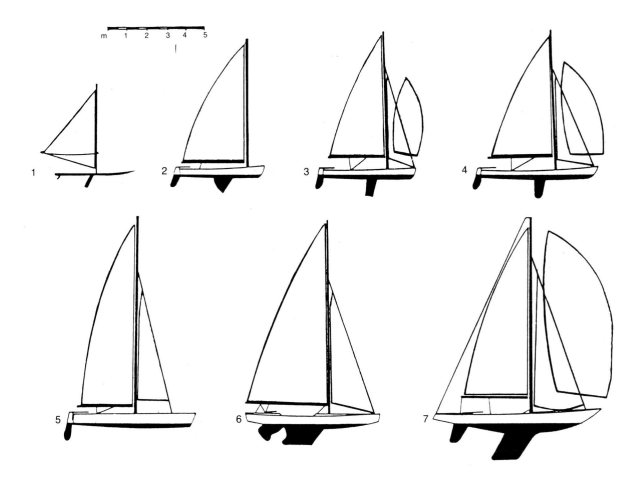

Table 3. Cost of the Olimpic Areas

AREA	SURFACE AREA		BASIC COSTS			PREPARATION COSTS		TOTAL COST
	TOTAL SURFACE	SURFACE AREA NOT DEVELOPED OR MADE INTO GARDENS	PURCHASE OR EXPROPIATION	TRANSFER OF SERVICES	DEVELOPMENT	GARDENS AND PARKS	PUBLIC SPACES	
Llobregat	1.022	913 Ha	35 M/Ha	2 M/Ha	2,5 M/Ha	10 M/Ha (5 Ha)	50 M/Ha (5 Ha)	
			4.565 M	1.826 M	2.282 M	1.500 M	250 M	10.423 M
Montjuïc	389	222		2,5 M/Ha	8 M/Ha	20 M/Ha (150)	100 M/Ha (15)	
				555 M	1.776 M	3.000 M	1.500 M	6.831 M
Parc de Mar (Poble Nou)	125	125	5 M/Ha	5 M/Ha	10 M/Ha	30 M/Ha (70)	100 M/Ha (15)	
			625 M	625 M	1.250 M	2.100 M	1.500 M	6.100 M
Diagonal	103	40	20 M/Ha	10 M/Ha	10 M/Ha	55 M/Ha (10)	100 M/Ha (19)	
			800 M	400 M	400 M	550 M	1.000 M	3.150 M
Vall d'Hebron	54	49	10 M/Ha	10 M/Ha	10 M/Ha (20)	30 M/Ha (10)	70 M/Ha (10)	
			490 M	390 M	490 M	600 M	700 M	2.770 M
Banyoles	—	30	—	2 M/Ha	5 M/Ha	20 M/Ha (10)	50 M/Ha (5 Ha)	
			—	60 M	150 M	200 M	250 M	600 M
Marina	—	40	—	2 M/Ha	5 M/Ha	20 M/Ha (10)	50 M/Ha (5 Ha)	
			—	80 M	200 M	200 M	250 M	730 M
Badalona-Montgat	—		—	—	—	—		
			—	—	—	750	750 M	1.500 M
Valles-Cerdanyola			—	—	—			
			—	—	—	1.250 M	1.250 M	2.500 M
TOTAL								34.664 M

FACILITIES

General criteria

Pasqual Maragall, Mayor of Barcelona, would like to see two dreams come true regarding the installations for the 1992 Olympic Games in Barcelona. He would like these installations to be model facilities in line with the strict but logical requirements of the International Olympic Committee, but he would also like them to be places where the athletes from all over the world can feel comfortable and happy as the success of the Games depends on their state of mind. Maragall would also like to add another kind of happiness to that already mentioned; he would like the installations to be a real sports university that may bring benefit to all sportsmen and women from all over Spain. For this reason the *Olympic Ring* on the mountain of Montjuïc has been designed and for this reason too a great many projects are underway to carry out alterations in other installations which are to serve as supports for the large sports complexes.

The new constructions and also the alterations carried out on the facilities which already exist, must fulfil the following requirements:

Optimize the sports conditions and bring them in line with the requirements of the International Federations. The latest technical advances will be incorporated into the construction of the facilities to help promote high performance sports, the making of records, the recognition of athletes and the spectacular nature of competition sport. As far as possible the new constructions will be situated inside parks and garden areas as the location and surroundings of the installations help to optimize conditions. The mountain of Montjuïc, which has a long, successful history in sporting events, is the ideal setting for the main complex.

To fulfil the functional requirements connected with an Olympic competition, such as: separate areas for the athletes, the members of the Organization, the guests of honour, the officials, the press, and the spectators; to have sufficient complementary services for the athletes and technical staff, the spectators, the guests of honour, and the press, radio, and television; complementary facilities for warming up, preparation and medical checks aimed at improving the athletes' performance; the shortest possible distance between the approaches and the warming up, competition, and service areas with orderly traffic along such corridors; to offer optimal visibility from all seats and also to provide information and control supports (screens, scoreboards, etc.) to allow the spectators to have the latest data on competition scores at all times; to provide excellent air-conditioning, lighting, security and safety measures, signs, etc.

To cover the quantitative and qualitative requirements of the Olympic Games. For this the necessary facilities must be built or adapted for the actual events and also for the training and preparation of the athletes. As far as possible the facilities will be concentrated in one area so that distances and travelling times to and from these installations and to and from the Olympic village are reduced to a minimum. The training areas should be as near as possible to the Olympic Village. There should be complementary facilities in the competition areas for use by the athletes either for training or for leisure purposes.

Good conditions for both spectators and those employed in the communication media as mentioned above but also including: inside a relatively restricted area, the possibility of choosing the events considered to be most interesting; easy access and suitable transport; pleasant surroundings –parks, gardens, views, etc.– which make walking around the installations an attrative experience; the architectonic quality of the installations and the complex in general making the role of uniqueness quite obvious; additional facilities, such as rest areas, restaurants, etc. It is also desirable for there to be other facilities in the area thus avoiding an isolated, segregated complex of sports areas.

To meet the relevant technical requirements with regard to the use of the facilities once the Games have finished, such as: acceptable maintenance costs; the number of spectator seats should be suitable for normal requirements and therefore part of the seating used for the Olympic events should be able to be dismantled easily; it should be possible to convert the provisional installations for the press and organization of the Games into other, more useful facilities; the facilities should be located in areas of the city or region which make their use after the Games viable, i.e. they should be in line with the projects aimed at improving living conditions in the area and at satisfying the requirements of the population; to promote the existing facilities by improving and diversifying the present supply of services.

The Olympic Village should be located in an area where it can later be used to provide housing in line with the requirements of urban restoration. The Olympic Village complex should help relieve the present stresses brought about by urban restoration and growth. Thus the installations to be used for the Olympic Games can easily be converted into facilities for everyday use: schools, clinics, shops, sports, cultural, and social facilities.

The solution adopted

It is possible to locate the various different Olympic facilities inside the municipal boundaries of the city of Barcelona as there are many sports installations coupled with a long history of organizing skills. This book deals with the hypothetical location of each of the Olympic competition and training centres. This does not mean that decisions have been taken for each of these centres. On the contrary, many of the facilities will most probably be substituted by other, better ones during the course of the work to be carried out. The detailed list of facilities given below should be taken as a first draft that may be corrected over the next few years. For the moment, however, this draft fulfils the requirements of the Olympic Office for a coherent criterion, a feasible cost, and locations suitable for the future development and equipment of the city. In effect, the choice of the competition and training facilities means:

Meeting the Olympic requirements by providing a larger number of facilities than is necessary so that a choice can later be made between them. Most Olympic competitions have been held in 30 or 35 different installations. This book gives a choice of 46 competition facilities, 45 for training and another 77 which could also be used for training. From these and those that will be built in the next few years, we are sure that a solution in line with the requirements of the International Federations will be found.

Giving priority to the criterion of making use of present facilities. Of the installations considered suitable for Olympic events, only 12 will be specially built. The remaining 34 only need to be improved or provisionally extended (with the exception of the Montjuïc stadium, which has to be completely renewed – see information relating to the Olympic Ring). Of the 45 training installations chosen; only 9 are to be built especially for the Games while the remaining 36 only need to have some improvements made to them, mainly in the flooring, dressing rooms, lighting, etc. The criterion of making use of the installations already in existence is not only economical but it is also in line with a large-scale project of urban restoration in which the facilities already in existence play an important role as they act as catalyzers for social relations, for long established customs, and for daily life in urban surroundings.

In many cases newly built facilities do not fit in with the surroundings and are not used sufficiently. For this reason the idea of building one enormous complex of sports facilities was discarded from the very beginning. Such a complex is an effective solution for the fortnight of the Games but afterwards would be an excessive burden on the city.

Building special facilities (Stadium, Sports Pavilion, Olympic Swimming Pool, Velodrome) which do not exist in Barcelona as yet. Apart from the holding of the Olympic Games, a city with over three million inhabitants should have facilities available for international competitions of all types. Barcelona has a strong, long-standing sporting tradition and occupies an important position in many competitions. The city should, therefore, make sure that it has those special facilities which make it possible to train and compete well and at the same time to provide the spectators with an interesting performance. These facilities should be available in the very near future. (The last construction of this type in Barcelona was the Picornell Swimming Pool in Montjuïc in 1970.)

Choosing temporary constructions for those sports, which, although they are important in the Olympic Games, will not usually become widely practised sports, such as, for example, boxing, weight lifting, judo, fencing, archery, etc. In the case of these sports the large areas necessary for the Olympic events would not be used sufficiently afterwards. The proposal, therefore, is to house them in existing buildings or open spaces so that the facilities can easily be converted back again to their original function.

In other cases temporary installations will be situated in existing parks or ones that have been new built but efforts will be made to ensure that later use and conservation are not affected.

Opting for a concentrated solution that will satisfy the Olympic requirements. At the same time, however, the facilities should be positioned in various different areas so that they cover the needs of a wide sector of the population after the Olympic Games. Almost all the competition facilities are concentrated in four areas around the Barcelona city centre: Parc de Mar, Montjuïc, Diagonal, and Valle Hebrón. The distances between these areas are very small: between 2 and 4 kilometres or between 5 and 15 minutes in public or private transport. These facilities do not include, of course, special installations, such as the marina, the rowing canal, canoeing on rapids, etc. The criteria used for choosing the areas mentioned are explained in detail on pages

Contributing to correcting the deficit of the existing facilities. The other facilities to be built, which are not considered to be special are all in line with a project to improve such installations in the worst equipped districts and areas, as expressed by the policy for sport of the Sports Department of the Barcelona City Council. In fact, all the new facilities, whether they are for competition or training purposes, will be functional at district level and will be used for school sports and to provide facilities for the general population as well as for training and actual competitions.

Implementing a general policy of improvements to existing facilities. The 36 different training facilities already in existence and the 80 alternative installations mentioned should be improved on to make them more profitable and in better condition. In accordance with the above mentioned criteria it is preferable to renovate and improve existing installations –wherever this is possible– rather than proceed to build new facilities.

Alongside each Olympic event, the most important requirements and the event facilities selected are shown. The event facilities are numbered from 1 upwards. The training facilities are also shown in the table and are numbered from 101. The last colum lists other facilities suitable for training and these are numbered from 201.

TABLE 4. Competition and Training Installations.

SPORT	REQUIREMENTS	FINAL COMPETITION PHASE	TOURNAMENT COMPETITIONS	TRAINING	OTHER TRAINING INSTALLATIONS
1. ATHLETICS	60.000 spectators, ampliable to 80.000 Inside of 400 m 2/3 km circuit; 20 km and 50 km walks Marathon 42,195 m Warming up: 1 400 m inside track 2 throwing fields Training areas: 4 complete 400 m tracks	1 Olympic Stadium of Montjuic 2 "Parc de Migdia" Circuit 3 Montjuic Circuit 4 Marathon Course *5 "Serrahima" Stadium *6 "Julià Capmany" *7 "La Fuixarda" Rugby Ground *8 "Serrahima" Stadium Throwing Field * Warming-up Installations	1 Olympic Stadium of Montjuic 2 "Parc de Migdia" Circuit 3 Montjuic Circuit 4 Marathon Course 5 "Serrahima" Stadium 6 "Julià Capmany" Stadium 7 "La Fuixarda" Rugby Ground 8 "Serrahima" Stadium Throwing Field	5 Serrahima Stadium 6 "Julià Capmany" Football Grounds 7 "La Fuixarda" Rugby Ground 8 "Serrahima" Stadium Throwing Field 101 Montjuic Swimming Club 102 F.C. Barcelona Athletics Track 103 Olympic Village Athletics Track 104 a University Sports Grounds b Hospitalet Municipal Sports Centre 105 Municipal Athletics Circuit Granollers 106 Cornellà Athletics Track	201 "Unió Esportiva Santboiana" 202 "Sagnier" Sports Grounds El Prat 203 Castelldefels Municipal Tracks 204 "Can Ferraté" Badalona 205 Mataró Municipal Stadium 206 "Can Rosès" Swimming Pool. Rubi 207 "St Oleguer" Swimming Pool. Sabadell 208 "St Oleguer 2" Circuit. Sabadell 209 "Can Jofresa" Circuit. Sabadell 210 St. Andreu de la Barca Municipal Circuit
2. BASKETBALL	15.000 spectators 26×14 m playing court 40×20 m total court 7 m minimum ceiling height Competition pavilions (2): 4-5.000 spectators Warming up areas: 2 30×18 m courts Training areas: 5 pavilions with 30×20 m courts	9 Olympic Sports Centre	10 "Palau Blaugrana I" 11 "Joventut de Badalona" Sports Centre	107 "St. Josep" Pavilion. Badalona 108 "La Salle Bonanova" Pavilion 109 "AES de Sarrià" Pavilion 110 "Blaugrana II" Pavilion 111 INEF Pavilion. Esplugues	211 "Font d'en Peixo" El Prat de Llobregat 212 Molins de Rei Mncpl. Pav. 213 Mollet del Vallès Mncpl. Pav. 214 "Les Moreres". Esplugues 215 "Can Caralleu" Centre 216 "La Parellada". St. Boi de bregat 217 "Les Planes". Hospitalet 218 "St. Ildefonso" Pav. Cornellà 219 St. Joan Despi Mncpl. Pav. 220 "Municipal Nou" Pav. Sta. Coloma de Gramenet
3. HANDBALL	15.000 spectators 40×20 m playing court 45×25 m total court 12.5 m minimum ceiling height 2 competition pavilions 5.000 spectators Warming up areas: 2 42×24 m rooms Training areas: 4/5 42×24 m rooms (h=12.5)	9 Olympic Sports Centre	12 Granollers Sports Centre 13 Mataró Sports Centre	112 "Espanya Industrial" Pav. 113 "Squash Barcelona" Pav. 114 "Llars Mundet" Pav. 115 University Sports Ground Pav.	221 Viladecans Mncpl. Pav. 222 Gavà Mncpl. Pav. 223 "Can Tusquets". St. Joan Despi 224 "Sta. Eulàlia". Hospitalet 225 Cerdanyola Mncpl. Pav. 226 Ripollet Mncpl. Sports Centre 227 St. Cugat Mncpl. Pav. 228 Sabadell Mncpl. Sports Centre 229 "Can San" Centre. Barcelona 230 "Bon Pastor" Centre. Barcelona

TABLE 4. Competition and Training Installations.

SPORT	REQUERIMENTS	FINAL PHASE COMPETITION	TOURNAMENT COMPETITIONS	TRAINING	OTHER TRAINING INSTALLATIONS
4. BOXING	15.000 spectators 6×6 m ring 8×8 m platform 17×17 m judges' area 1 competicion pavilion 5.000 spectators 6 warming up rings 16/18 sparring rings	9 Olympic Sports Centre	14 Mncpl. Sports Centre. Barcelona	116 "Unió Esportiva Horta" 117 Esplugues Mncpl. Pav. 118 St. Just Mncpl. Pav. 119 Hospitalet Mncpl. Pav. 14 Barcelona Mncpl. Sports Centre	The installations from 211 to 230 are usable
5. CYCLING	4-7.500 spectators 250 m/333.33 m inside 1 4×25 km level circuit 3.000 spectators 1 180 km circuit. 15/25 kms per lap	15 "Vall d'Hebró" Cycle Track 16 Road Race Cycle Track 17 Road Race	15 "Vall d'Hebró" Cycle Track 16 Road Race Cycle Track 17 Road Race	15 "Vall d'Hebró" Cycle Track 16 Road Race Cycle Track 17 Road Race	231 Igualada Cycle Track * 232 Mataró Cycle Track * 233 Lleida Cycle Track * 234 El Vendrell Cycle Track * * After refurbishing.
6. FENCING	1.300/3.000 spectators 2×14 m fencing area 6×21 m raised platform 10 6×21 courts 9 warming up courts 30/40 training courts	18 Blaugrana Ice Rink	18 Blaugrana Ice Rink	18 Blaugrana Ice Rink 120 Alfonso XIII Sports Centre	No other installations will be necessary
7. FOOTBALL	75.000 spectators 1 100/110×64/75 m field 5 tournament stadiums 15/30.000 spectators Preparation: 5 fields	19 "Camp Nou" Stadium	19 "Camp Nou" Stadium 20 R.C.D. Español Stadium 21 F.C. Barcelona Mini-stadium 22 "Creu Alta" Stadium. Sabadell 23 "Hospitalet" Stadium The possibility of using the 1982 World Cup stadiums will be looked into.	121 St. Andreu. Barcelona 122 St. Boi Football Club 123 Camp Nou II. Barcelona 124 Granollers Football Club 125 Terrassa Football Club	235 Cornellà Mncpl. Stadium 236 Badalona Football Club
8. GYMNASTICS	12.000 spectators 73×33.5 m open area Individual rooms with video Warming up: 1 Gimnasium, 1 complete set of apparatus Training: 10/13 sets of apparatus	9 Olympic Sports Centre	9 Olympic Sports Centre	126 "La Fuixarda" Gymnasium 127 Olympic Sports Centre Training Areas 128 "Parc Vall d'Hebró" Gymnasium 129 St. Feliu de Llobregat Sports Centre	237 Montjuïc Pav. 238 Barcelona Swimming Club 239 Granollers Pav. 240 Vilanova i la Geltrú Pav. 241 Barcelona Mncpl. Gymnasium

TABLE 4. Competition and Training Installations.

SPORT	REQUERIMENTS	FINAL PHASE COMPETITION	TOURNAMENT COMPETITIONS	TRAINING	OTHER TRAINING INSTALLATIONS
9. WEIGHTLIFTING	5.000 seats 1 3×3 m lifting area 1 4×4 platform 18 weightlifting exercise rooms rest areas 4/8 3×3 m pre-warm up podiums 40 3×3 m training podiums	24 Renfe-Meridiana Pav.	24 Renfe-Meridiana Pav.	130 Victoria Eugenia Sports Centre	No other installations will be necessary
10. EQUESTRIAN SPORTS	2(20×60) m. 3.000 spectators 1(100×80) m. 10.000 spectators 7.695 m circuits 1.800 m course 6 & 10 km routes 6(20×60) m warming up areas 4/5(100×50) m. 10 runs Training: 1 gallop track, 2(20×60) pavs.	25 Club de Polo Riding Club 26 Equestrian Run 19 "Camp Nou" Stadium. F.C. Barcelona (Nations' Cup)	25 Club de Polo Riding Club 26 Equestrian Run 19 "Camp Nou" Stadium. F.C. Barcelona (Nations' Cup)	25 Club de Polo Riding Club 131 Riding Circuits	242 "La Fuixarda" Riding School 243 Babieca Riding School (Viladecans) 244 Open Tennis. El Prat
11. FIELD HOCKEY	5.000 & 10.000 spectators 2 91.5×55 m artificial turf Training: 3 91.5×55 m Warming up: 1 91.5×55 m (the field used in competitions)	27 Terrassa Mncpl. Hockey Stadium 28 Campo del Egara. Pla del Bonaire. Terrassa 29 Pau Negre Stadium. Barcelona	27 Terrassa Mncpl. Hockey Stadium 28 Campo del Egara. Pla del Bonaire. Terrassa 29 Pau Negre Stadium. Barcelona	132 R.C. Polo Barcelona 133 Sant Cugat Junior 27 Terrassa Mncpl. Hockey Stadium 28 Campo del Egara. Pla del Bonaire. Terrassa 29 Pau Negre Stadium. Barcelona	245 St. Andreu de la Barca. Mncpl. Circuits 246 Esplugues Mncpl. Sports Ground 247 Terrassa Sports Club. Les Pedritxes. Matadepera 248 "Can Sala". Terrassa 249 St. Quirze de la Serra Mncpl. Sports Ground
12. JUDO	10-7.000 spectators 16×16 m tatami mats 22.5×22.5 platform 1.15 m high Training: 16 tatami mats Warming up: 2 tatami mats 16×16 m	30 Hospitalet Sports Centre	30 Hospitalet Sports Centre	134 Metallurgy Pavilion	The installations from 211 to 230 are usable

TABLE 4. Competition and Training Installations.

SPORT	REQUIREMENTS	FINAL COMPETITION PHASE	TOURNAMENT COMPETITIONS	TRAINING	OTHER TRAINING INSTALLATIONS
13. WRESTLING	7-8.000 spectators 1 12×12 mat 64×16 podium (4 mats) Warming up: 3/4 mats Training 16 mats	31 "Mercat del Peix"	31 "Mercat del Peix"	135 Barcelona Trade Fair. No. 1 Pavilion	The installations from 211 to 230 are usable
14. SWIMMING & DIVING	10.000 spectators Swimming: 50×25 m Diving: 20×20 m Warming up: 25×33.3 m Training: 3 jumps	32 "Bernat Picornell" Swimming Pools (Swimming & Diving) 33 Olympic Pool "Parc de Mar" (Swimming & Diving) 34 Sant Jordi Pool (Relay Races)	32 "Bernat Picornell" Swimming Pools 33 "Parc de Mar" Olympic Pool 34a Sant Jordi Pool 34b C.N. Barcelona	34b Barcelona C.N. 136 C.N. Sabadell (Swimming & Diving) 137 C.N. Mataró (Swimming & Diving) 138 C.N. Granollers (Swimming & Diving) 139 C.N. Montjuic (Swimming) 140 "Llars Mundet" Pool (Relays) 141 "Guinardó" Pool (Relays)	250 Castelldefels Sports Centre 251 "Can Mercader". Cornella 252 Hospitalet Mncpl. Pool 253 Montcada i Reixac Mncpl. Installations 254 Sta. Perpètua de Moguda Mncpl. Installations 255 Rubí Mncpl. Pool 256 Terrassa Mncpl. Pool 257 INEF Pools. Esplugues 258 St. Vicenç dels Horts Mncpl. Pool
15. PENTATHLON	1 pentathlon course The rest of the sports installations Riding: 800 m Fencing 4.000 m course 60 m slope Shooting: 20 shots at moving target	18 Blaugrana Ice Rink 25 R.C. Polo Gallop Course 32 "Bernat Picornell" Swimming Pools 33 "Parc de Mar" Olympic Pool 36 Pentathlon Course 35a Llobregat Shooting Range 35b "Argentona Mataró" Shooting Range		Those corresponding to each specialty	Those corresponding to each specialty
16. CANOEING (Rapids)	600 m slalom with 25/30 gates	37a Noguera Pallaresa (Escaló-La Pobla) 37b Valira (La Seu d'Urgell) 37c Garona (Lés-Bossost)	37a Noguera Pallaresa (Escaló-La Pobla) 37b Valira (La Seu d'Urgell) 37c Garona (Lés-Bossost)	37a Noguera Pallaresa (Escaló-La Pobla) 37b Valira (La Seu d'Urgell) 37c Garona (Lés-Bossost)	

TABLE 4. Competition and Training Installations.

SPORT	REQUIREMENTS	FINAL COMPETITION PHASE	TOURNAMENT COMPETITIONS	TRAINING	OTHER TRAINING INSTALLATIONS
17. ROWING & KAYAKING (Calm water)	2.300×110 m Regata Canal min. 3 m depth 10.000 spectators Pre-warming up: 1 swimming pool & 1 gymnasium The same installation & 2 other training canals	38a Lake Banyoles 38b Llobregat Canal	38a Lake Banyoles 38b Llobregat Canal	142 Mequinenza Reservoir (2 canals)	No other installations will be necessary
10. TENNIS	8-10.000 spectators 23.77×10.97 m court with 36.5×18.5 m margins 2 courts/3.000 spectators Warming up: 6 courts/1.000 spectators 20 training & warming up courts	39 R.C. Tennis. Barcelona	39 R.C. Tennis. Barcelona 40 R.C. de Polo. Barcelona 41 Tennis Turó. Barcelona	39 R.C. Tennis. Barcelona 40 R.C. de Polo. Barcelona 41 Tennis Turó. Barcelona	259 C.T. Andrés Gimeno. Castelldefels 260 C.T. La Salud 261 C.D. Hispano Francès 262 C.T. Castelldefels 263 T.C. Badalona 264 Círculo Sabadellés 265 C.T. Granvia 266 C.T. Mataró 267 C.N. Sant Cugat 268 C.T. San Gervasio 269 C.D. Laietano 270 C.T. Barcino 271 C.T. Pompeia 272 C.N. Montjuïc
19. TABLE TENNIS	3-5.000 spectators Tables with 14×7 m margins Warming up: 6 tables of 10×20 m 20 training tables	42 Montjuïc Palacio Nacional	42 Montjuïc Palacio Nacional	42 Montjuïc Palacio Nacional	No other installations will be necessary
20. ARCHERY	1.000-2.000 spectators 150×60 m range 230×70 security area Warming up: 20×40 m pavilion Training: the competition range	43a University Sports Ground 43b "Parc del Llobregat" Archery	43a University Sports Ground 43b "Parc del Llobregat" Archery	43a University Sports Ground 43b "Parc del Llobregat" Archery	No other installations will be necessary

TABLE 4. Competition and Training Installations.

SPORT	REQUIREMENTS	FINAL COMPETITION PHASE	TOURNAMENT COMPETITIONS	TRAINING	OTHER TRAINING INSTALLATIONS
21. SHOOTING	3.000 spectators Trapshooting Skeet Shooting Moving Target (Running Boar) Velocity of 25.5 m Warming up: the same installation Training: the same installation	35a Argentona-Mataró Shooting Range 35b "Parc del Llobregat" Range	35a Argentona-Mataró Shooting Range 35b "Parc del Llobregat" Range	143 Montjuïc Olympic Range	No other installations will be necessary
22. SAILING		44 Pleasure Harbour	44 Pleasure Harbour	44 Pleasure Harbour	No other installations will be necessary
20. VOLLEYBALL	15-17.000 spectators 18×9 m court with margins to 34×20 h=12.5 m 5.000 spectators Warming up: 2 rooms Training 4 courts 2×20×20	9 Olympic Sports Centre	45 "Parc de Mar" Sports Centre 46 "Par Vall d'Hebró" Pavilion	144 "La Caixa" Pavilion 145 C.D. Hispano Francés Pavilion	273 "La Plana" Sports Centre. Badalona 274 "C. Junior" Pavilion. Sant Cugat 275 St. Andreu de la Barca Mncpl. Pavilion 276 Martorell Mncpl. Pavilion 277 "Vallpark" Pavilion
24. WATER POLO	5-10.000 spectators 33×20 swimming pool Warming up: the same pool or one of 25×20 m Training 4/5 pools 33×16.6 m	32 "Bernat Picornell" Pools 33 "Parc de Mar" Olympic Pool	32 "Bernat Picornell" Pools 33 "Parc de Mar" Olympic Pool	136 C.N. Sabadell 137 C.N. Mataró 138 C.N. Granollers 140 "Llars Mundet" Pool 141 Guinardó Pool 39b C.N. Barcelona	

Athletics

The facilities will be based in the Olympic Stadium, with a seating capacity of at least 60,000 which could be extended to 80,000 (5,000 VIP's and 2,000 journalists and officials) with all the necessary services. There will be a reglamentary 400 metre, 8 lane track, and areas for pole vault, high jump, long jump, and triple jump. All the tracks will be made of approved synthetic material. The area inside the track will be grass and will measure 105 × 68, with areas for shot put, throwing the hammer, javelin, and discus. Three more circuits (for the 20 and 50 km walking events and the marathon) with asphalted tracks will also be designed along with training areas near the stadium, with a 400 metre, 8 lane track, areas for long jump and high jump, and three other areas for the throwing events training. There will also be another four or five training stadiums for the various teams taking part in the Games.

In order to fulfil the above mentioned requirements, the Montjuïc stadium is to be altered and made into an Olympic Stadium. There are various possibilities for the other requirements, as shown in the table 4. The present stadium, which occupies an important position in the Montjuïc Olympic Ring complex, will be completely renovated. This renovation process is being implemented after putting out an international tender for projects on 10th August 1983, the results of which were announced in January of this year.

This project is considered to be one of the most important as far as use of the facilities after the Games is concerned. The Olympic Stadium will fulfil a triple function in this respect. Firstly, the facilities, services, and seating capacity will make the Montjuïc Stadium the only really large stadium in Catalonia and it will be able to be used for all types of athletics meetings. Secondly, the stadium is one of the facilities which will later make up a large physical education centre. The centre will be located in the building which will serve as an ancillary press centre during the Olympic Games and will co-ordinate and implement the facilities of the Olympic Ring. This teaching facility will be available not only to the students of the physical education centre but also to schoolchildren who wish to take up athletics for competition purposes. Thirdly, the installations will be able to serve as training centres for athletes who are members of clubs or who are directly affiliated to the various sport federations. For some of the walking routes city streets will have to be used but these can be closed to traffic at weekends and used for training, jogging, cycling, etc. These will be normal activities for those who use the Montjuïc Park where these circuits are located.

Basketball

Basketball, which in the last three years has become almost as popular as football in Spain, will be one of the most attractive events of the 1992 Olympic Games. The knockout rounds for this event should be held in one or two pavilions, preferably not together with other events owing to the number of teams involved. At any rate the finals should be held where the seating capacity is largest because of the popularity this sport has reached. All the pavilions will have stands reserved for the press, VIP's, athletes, and officials. They will also have all the necessary services to attend the public and the media.

Barcelona is well able to fulfil all the requirements as can be seen from the table of facilities. Barcelona has been very important in the recent boom of basketball in Spain and has several clubs in the Spanish league. The new Olympic Sports Pavilion, situated in the Olympic Ring near the Stadium will become the centre of attention for this event. This pavilion, financed almost completely by the Delegation of Barcelona, will be complemented by the Blaugrana Pavilion, of the Football Club Barcelona, and the pavilion of the Joventut team of Badalona, one of the most famous clubs in Spanish basketball.

After the Olympic Games have finished, these installations will continue to fulfil the same functions as before the Games. The Olympic Pavilion will carry out teaching, training, and competition functions in a similar way to the installations comprising the Olympic Ring, which will be co-ordinated and directed by the new physical education centre. The three warming up rooms will be mainly used for teaching and training, although some local competitions may occasionally be held there. The main hall of the Pavilion will also be suitable for holding conferences, concerts, etc.

Handball

The Olympic requirements for handball are very similar to those for basketball. The facilities provided then will also be similar. The Olympic Stadium will be used for the finals while other facilities, in addition to those used for the basketball knockouts, will be used for the first part of the competition. If the Barcelona or Joventut pavilions can be used for basketball, then installations, such as Granollers –the cradle of Catalan handball– and Mataró can be used for handball. With some renovation work these installations would be ideal for Olympic handball.

Regarding the use of the facilities after the Game, they will function as before, but perhaps with an even better substructure.

Boxing

For this event large capacity halls are usually used where the basketball, handball or volleyball finals have been held along with the gymnastics knockout rounds. Owing to the time the event lasts (14 days with all the knockouts), it would seem to be advisable to give over one pavilion for this event exclusively. The Barcelona Municipal Sports Pavilion, in the Carrer Lleida on Montjuïc, is suitable for this event, with very few alterations. The seating capacity here would be 7,500. Separate access will be available for those seated on the platform of honour and all the necessary requirements will be fulfilled. The Olympic Pavilion will be used for the finals of all the categories.

Both the Municipal Sports Pavilion in the Carrer Lleida and the training facilities shown in the table are in operation at the present time and are used for competitions, shows, and training purposes. Any modifications which may be carried out to make them more suitable for the Olympics will also constitute an improvement for normal use but their actual functions will remain unvaried.

Cycling

For the track events the new velodrome in the Valle Hebrón is completely finished. This velodrome will be used for the world track cycling championships to be held in Barcelona in August 1984. The installations are situated to the south of the Labyrinth Park, near the Valle Hebrón Park and there are excellent approaches from the Second Ring Road.

The main features of the velodrome are: 250 m track in Doussier Afzela wood from Cameroon, nominal track width –7 m, over 0.60 of blue band. The installation will initially be open air but the possibility of closing it in exists. The permanent seating capacity is 4,000 but can be increased to 7,500 by using easy to assemble extra seating. The surface area is about 4,000 m² with 2,000 m² taken up with seating. The central area is about 3,000 m². The maximum superelevation is 41.5° and the minimum 12°. There are dressing rooms, showers, warehouses, bicycle sheds, workshop, gymnasium, medical service, i.e. all the services necessary for the athletes, spectators, communication media, etc. are provided.

The are two possibilities available for the circuits. One is to use the B-30 - A-7 motorway for the 100 km team event. Service lanes are available all along this motorway which would allow the traffic to continue circulating while the event is taking place. The 180 km circuit, on ordinary roads, would have its starting point at the velodrome and would run through the Tibidabo Park and the Vallés area.

The velodrome will continue to be used mainly by the Cycling Federation for training and competition purposes. The Barcelona City Council is going to schedule activies for the velodrome all year round.

Fencing

Both the preliminary rounds and the finals can be held in one set of installations of a suitable size. One or two floors will be located in a preferential position on an elevated platform measuring 6 × 21 metres. The steel floor, measuring 14 × 2 metres, will be located in the centre. There will be 10 additional floors of the same size for preliminary rounds and another 9 for warming up. Barcelona has the necessary installations for the fencing events. The whole competition could be run in the Ice Rink of the Football Club Barcelona, located in the Diagonal area. The floor measures 61 × 26 metres and would house the areas necessary for the finals and also all those for the preliminary rounds and warming up sessions. The pavilion has all the necessary services and a seating capacity of 1,300. This could be increased to 3,000 with temporary seating or in the Alfonso XII Pavilion in the Montjuïc area, which fulfils all the conditions.

Once the fencing installations have been disassembled, the Ice Rink or the Alfonso XII Pavilion can the return to their normal function: ice-skating and ice-hockey and exhibition hall respectively.

Football

4 or 5 stadiums with a seating capacity of between 15,000 and 30,000 will be needed for the preliminary rounds. For the finals a large stadium with a seating capacity of over 75,000 will be necessary. There is no doubt that Barcelona has facilities available to cover this demand amply. The table of facilities gives details of these installations. All the stadiums mentioned fulfil the requirements for event and training purposes amply.

Gymnastics

All the gymnastics events are usually held in one pavilion with a seating capacity in excess of 17,000. The floor size should be 73 × 33.5 metres and all the apparatus should be able to be arranged at the same time. A separate room is required for warming up and should have all the necessary apparatus. There should also be an auxiliary gymnasium and individual rooms with videos. Training will be done in one or more pavilions with a total of 10 sets of apparatus.

The Olympic Pavilion will be Barcelona's solution to the Olympic requirements for this event. Warming up rooms are included in the project for this building. The function of this building after the Olympics has already been described above. The training rooms –which also feature in the table of facilities– would return to urban use.

Weight lifting

All the weight lifting events are usually held in one sports pavilion with a seating capacity of around 5,000. As in the other installations, a platform should be reserved for guests of honour, the press, and athletes. The competition podium will be situated in a central position and will be 4 × 4 metres in size. Near this central podium there will be between 4 and 8 others for warming up, along with a gymnasium for muscle exercising, 15-20 rest cubicles, dressing rooms, massage rooms, weighing room, judges' room, sanitary installations, etc. For training an area with about 40 podiums measuring 3 × 3 metres will also be needed.

The proposal is to hold the weight lifting events in a new pavilion to be build in the next few years in the RENFE-Meridiana area, which will be of the necessary size to comply with the regulations for weight lifting. After the Games the pavilion can be used for many different sports and will serve the area.

Horse riding

There are three Olympic horse riding events: dressage, show jumping, and racing. It is advisable to have all the horse riding events in the same installations. This is also advisable from the point of view of box concentration and services for the horses. It is also better for the judges to be able to stay in the installations.

The riding facilities of the Real Club de Polo —situated in the Diagonal area— will be used. The capacity here is 3,000 spectators and 1,000 participants and all the public services are already available, with a control tower and a waiting area measuring 80 × 42 metres. The Nations Cup show jumping competition will be held as one of the closing events of the Olympic Games. The Camp Nou, the Football Club Barcelona football stadium, with a capacity of 114,000, will be used for this. It is easily reached from the boxes of the Real Club de Polo as all that has to be done is to cross the road. Four routes will be devised for the racing events: 2 of them in the city park of Collserola and two more in the Diagonal area.

The Real Club de Polo has about 400 boxes with training areas measuring 120 × 80 metres, a bowling green measuring 59 × 49 metres, 2 swimming pools measuring 20 × 10 and 20 × 12.5 respectively, and a gymnasium measuring 10 × 25 metres which could be used by the participants. There are also two covered pavilions measuring 35 × 14 and 42.5 × 13.5 respectively for training and exercising the horses. Some necessary modifications will be carried out in this club to improve its present features. Its functions, however, will remain the same.

Hockey

A minimum of two synthetic grass hockey fields, measuring 91.5 × 55 metres and with 3 metre protection strips for the sides and 5 metres for the goal areas, will be necessary for this event. The field chosen for the finals of this event must have a capacity of at least 20,000. The second field should have a capacity of around 5,000. Another field of the same size will also be necessary for warming up purposes and should be situated near the other two. If Badalona is essential in scheduling the Olympic basketball events, then Terrassa will be crucial for hockey. A municipal Hockey Stadium for the "Can Jofresa" sports Area is in the project stage. The Egara field (Pla del Bonaire), the "Atletic" field (Can Salas), the present municipal stadium, and the Terrassa Sports Club field in Matadepera all have similar features. All these facilities could be temporarily extended to take between, 7,000 and 10,000 spectators. The present services could be modified to tie in with the Olympic requirements. The Pau Negre Stadium in Montjuïc will change its position within the Olympic Ring to allow for the construction of the Olympic Sports Pavilion. In its new position within the Olympic Ring the Pau Negre Stadium will be better orientated and will be able to incorporate temporary seating for 5,000 to 7,000 spectators. There are, therefore, five suitable stadiums with similar features which would cover the requirements for the preliminary rounds and the finals of this event.

For all the stadiums mentioned above work to replace the natural grass with the synthetic type will take place whether or not Barcelona is accepted as the host city for the 1992 Olympic Games. The temporary improvements and extensions will not change their present function.

Judo

All the judo events will take place in one pavilion with a seating capacity of 7,000-10,000. There will be a platform measuring 22.5 × 20.5 metres positioned about one metre above the level of the floor on which the tatami measuring 16 × 16 metres will be placed. Other tatamis of the same size will be positioned nearby for warming up purposes. The new municipal sports complex which is being built in Hospitalet and which will be incorporated into the Diagonal area, will have a room of a suitable size for judo competitions. When the Games have finished, these facilities and others mentioned for this event in the facilities table will revert to their normal functions after the temporary seating has been dismantled.

Wrestling

The requirements for the wrestling events are similar to those for judo: capacity for 7,000-8,000 spectators, and 64 × 16 metre podium, with four wrestling mats measuring 12 × 12 metres. Another 3 or 4 mats are necessary for warming up purposes.

The provisional nature of competition facilities for events such as wrestling or judo make it advisable to use a container building conditioned specifically for the Olympic Games, which could then revert to normal use afterwards. We would suggest using the Mercat de Peix as this building is a large, undivided structure covering 4,000 m². It is located in the Poble Nou area and very shortly a tender will be put out for the adaptation of this building for sport facilities as it is no longer used as a fish market. This old market will therefore be put to use in the world of sport both before and after the Olympic Games.

Swimming

Swimming is one of the most popular events of the Olympic Games. The most important facilities for the swimming events are: an Olympic pool, a diving pool and a warming up pool. The Olympic pool should be 50 metres long, 2.5 metres deep and at least 21 metres wide, although it is recommended that the width be 25 metres. The diving pool should measure at least 21 × 20 and be 5 metres deep. The warming up pool should also be 50 metres long and 12.5 metres wide. Synchro swimming can be carried out in the Olympic pool itself. The swimming pool complex does not necessarily have to closed in but it must house a minimum of 10,000 spectators, with a special platform reserved for VIP's, athletes, etc.

Barcelona offers two solutions for the swimming and diving events. The first is the Olympic pool or pool complex in the Parc de Mar, which is located in the Parc de Mar area near the Olympic Village. This would be an open-air swimming pool with provisional seating for 10,000 spectators. The swimming pool would measure 25 × 20 metres, the diving pool 25 × 20 metres and the warming up pool 50 × 12.5 metres. The situation of this swimming pool complex on the seafront in the Poble Nou area is very convenient for use after the Games as these southern and central districts of Barcelona are very lacking in this kind of facility. The second solution is the Bernardo Picornell swimming pool complex in the Olympic Ring on Montjuïc. This complex could house an Olympic level event if a few alterations were carried out, e.g. the modernization of the overflow system and increasing the present width of 22 metres to 25. A third possibility is the Sant Jordi swimming pool, which is due to be renovated very shortly. This pool could be used for the synchro swimming preliminary rounds. The remaining installations are shown on the table.

After the Games the Picornell swimming pools will be used by the physical education centre for training and competition purposes. The pool complex to be built in the Parc de Mar will later be used for schools and the general public. The Sant Jordi pool is situated in the heart of the Eixample and occupies a strategic position. It would be difficult to find a substitute for this pool as undeveloped land of this size is extremely hard to come by in the centre of Barcelona.

Modern Pentathlon

Each of the disciplines in the Pentathlon will be staged in the respective event areas: horse riding, fencing, shooting, and swimming. Only the 4,000 metres running –the last discipline in the modern pentathlon– will need a specific circuit. The facilities available for the Pentathlon are: the Real Club de Polo (horse riding), the Bernardo Picornell swimming pools or the Parc de Mar swimming pool complex (swimming), the Olympic Shooting range, in the Llobregat area, or the shooting area between Argentona and Mataró (shooting). For the 4,000 running we would sugguest the Diagonal area, with the Real Club de Polo as the starting and finishing points.

Canoeing (white water racing)

The canoe slalom and the downhill white water race will require natural facilities –stream or river– with special features which are often difficult to find. An artificial route can be built (as in the case of Munich) by taking advantage of drop in level of an existing canal. Barcelona has rejected the possibility of building an artificial canal for the canoeing event as the possibilities offered by the existing rivers are not sufficient. There are, however, excellent natural routes in the Pyrenees which could be used with some modifications to the surroundings. A few examples are: Noguera-Pallaresa (Escaló-Pobla); Valira (Seu d'Urgell) or Garonne (Lés Bossost). These routes would have to be analyzed and judged by the International Federation so that the relevant decisions can be taken. All three areas have been used for international competitions. When the chosen route has been properly prepared and the auxiliary facilities have been built, it can be made into a permanent canoeing centre.

Rowing and canoeing (flat water racing)

These events will be held on a regatta canal –either natural or artificial– in line with the Olympic requirements. According to the International Federations for rowing and canoeing these requirements are: still waters without currents; the banks should absorb the waves; the surroundings should protect from the wind as much as possible; there should be no obstacle (either natural or artificial) which could create unequal conditions along the route; the perimeter should be suitable for the trainers to travel along on bicycles; there should be markers, and also referee stations every 250 metres; photo-finish facilities on the finishing line; a nine metre high tower for giving the signal to start the race; movable aligning devices at 2,000, 1,000 and 500 metres, and a small marina for 12 small, motor driven boats. The canal should be at least 3 metres deep, if the bed is uneven. The recommended length is 2,100 metres and the minimum width 95 metres.

At present there is no canal either in or around Barcelona with these features. There are two possibilities for the staging of this event: a) Lake Banyoles, in Girona, which could easily be adapted to fulfil the requirements of an Olympic rowing event. Owing to its long sporting tradition this installation is well able to organize the event. b) The construction of a an artificial Olympic rowing canal in the Llobregat area.

The best solution would appear to that of Lake Banyoles, situated at 17 kilometres from Girona and 117 from Barcelona. The perimeter measures 7.720 metres. There is an excellent walkway all around the lake. The total length is 2,156 metres and the maximum width is 774 metres. The depth varies but at all points of the rowing canal it is at least the reglamentary 3 metres. The waters are calm with no current at all. When the Olympic Games have finished the lake will continue to be used for rowing and canoeing competition and training purposes, in addition to the other water sports practised at the present time:

water-skiing and swimming. The new auxiliary constructions will give wider scope to the present facilities. It will be possible to organize stays all the year round for rowing and canoeing teams —national and international— in excellent training conditions. The residential complexes built for the Olympic participants will later be sold as dwellings. Because of their size and capacity these dwellings will quickly become absorbed as a profitable investment by the urban communities.

Tennis

The main installation required for tennis is a court measuring 23.77 × 10.97 metres inside a rectangular area measuring at least 36.5 × 18.5 metres, with permanent or temporary seating for between 8,000 and 10,000 spectators. The flooring requirements have varied greatly worldwide in recent years and must be approved by the International Tennis Federation. Near this centre court there should be 2 other courts with similar features but with a seating capacity of 3,000, and another 6 courts with a seating capacity of 1,000. 20 more courts would be necessary for training and warming up.

The people of Barcelona will remember the exciting preliminary rounds of Davis Cup during the time of Manolo Santana, Juan Gisbert, and José Luis Arilla. The court used then was the *Talisman* court of the Real Club de Tenis of Barcelona. At present this court has a seating capacity of 5,500 which can easily be increased to 10,000. The same club has another 19 courts where one phase of the preliminary rounds could be held. The remaining preliminary rounds could be held in the Real Club de Polo, with 31 courts, and the Turó Tennis Club, with 18 courts. All these clubs are situated in the Diagonal area, are very near to one another, and have many complementary and social facilities.

All the tennis courts mentioned —and also those featured in the table of facilities— are already in existence and their use for the Olympic Games will not alter their normal function.

Table Tennis

Here a large room with 12 tables, with a space of 14 × 6 metres for each, is needed plus a central table with a space of 14 × 7 metres. About 20 tables will be needed for training purposes. Both the finals and the preliminaries could be played in the same room, which would have a seating capacity of 5,000 to 10,000 spectators. We suggest preparing the elliptical room of the Palau Nacional on Montjuïc for the preliminaries and also the finals. After the Games have finished, the Palace would revert to normal use.

Archery

The archery ground can be another temporary installation. All that is needed is grass surface of sufficient size for the men's event (70 metres wide × 90 metres long) and the women's event (60 metres wide × 70 metres long). Safety distances on either side of the lanes and behind the targets must also be taken into account.

The archers should be facing north and there should be a dark, uniform background behind the targets. This could be a line of trees or higher level ground with uniform grass.

At present there are no facilities of this kind in Barcelona. The proposal is to situate the archery ground in the Diagonal area on land lying between the boundaries of Barcelona, l'Hospitalet, and Esplugues. This land is classified as green belt and has not been developed. An alternative location would be the future Llobregat Park which will have large flat areas that could be set out in such as way as to fulfil the requirements for Olympic archery.

Olympic Shooting

The different Olympic shooting events and the installations required are: *trapshooting* –the size of the installation depends on the safety areas affected by the shots. This event should take place away from inhabited areas because of the high noise level. *Olympic Skeet* –the installation is a circular sector shape bounded by 36.8 metre rope over a circle with a radius of 19.2 metres. *Snap shooting* –the shooting distance for pistol range, standard pistol, large calibre, and ladies' pistol is 25 metres. The distance between the spectators and the shooting line is at least 5 metres. *Other pistol events* –the size and characteristics of the ranges are similar to those described above. The targets are linked in groups of 3 or 4 and work simultaneously. Each target corresponds to a shooting position. *Target shooting* –the shooting distance is 50 metres minimum. *Rifle Shooting* –the size of the installation depends on the shooting distance, which is 50 metres. *Moving Target* –The shooting distance is 50 metres and the general specifications are the same as for target shooting or silhouettes, the only difference being that the target can move horizontally in both directions. *Air pistol target shooting* –The shooting distance is 10 metres. A minimum of 10 targets are installed and are centred to each shooting position. *Air rifle target shooting* –The shooting distance is 10 metres. This range can be built in the open air but, as in the case of air pistol target shooting, it is advisable to close the range in.

Barcelona has no suitable facilities at present for the Olympic shooting events. The present Olympic shooting facilities on Montjuïc could only be used as training areas unless they were extended to cover the requirements of the Games. A new set of installations would have to be built, therefore, within Barcelona but at a suitable distance from residential areas. One of the possible locations would be the Llobregat Park, which is easily reached from the city, and the Maresme.

Sailing

The number of participants per class will be approximately: Soling (25), Starr (22), Flying Dutchman (28-30), Finn (40-45), Tornado (19-20), 470 (40-45), and Windsurfing (40-45). All these Olympic classes are light sailing classes, except. perhaps, in the case of the Soling. A distinction is thus made between these light sailing vessels and cruisers (vessels with a cabin) which require more port service. In the last Olympics some of the classes had their vessels in the water permanently while other were taken onto land after each regatta. The types of vessels change but the port and auxiliary services remain almost the same.

This study, at the preliminary project stage, proposes the use of the Catalan coast. This does not rule out the possibility of holding the sailing events somewhere else along the Mediterranean coast after suitable studies have been made at a later date. As the work is based in Catalonia it is worth mentioning that the Catalan shoreline measures 595 kilometres and has sandy beaches, rocky and cliff-lined coasts. At the present time, Catalonia has more boating facilities than any other Autonomous Community of the Spanish state. About 35 % per cent of Spanish sports and leisure vessels are to be found in Catalonia. There are 34 permannent marinas and also other smaller installations along the Catalan coast.

These facilities provide a total of 10,831 moorings, about 35 % of the total available in Spain. Taking only heavy or light marinas into account the main figures are: 10,831 moorings in service, 1,000 under construction, 900 moorings authorized or in the process of being authorized, over 3,000 new moorings.

Many of the existing ports and marinas could be used for the Olympic Games if some modifications were made. A new Olympic Marina could also be built. This would not involve an enormous additional cost as, in view of the demand for more moorings, it would be worth considering giving over the project to the private sector. The prestige and publicity such a port would get as the Olympic port would be sufficient to encourage private promoters to carry out the work. The conditions of the coastline where the regattas are to be held are also important as well as those of the port itself. Areas with very little wind should be avoided as should those with high cliffs which may affect the direction of the wind. Areas with currents,

PALMA DE MALLORCA

Table 5				
		BOATING CLUBS IN CATALUNYA AND PALMA DE MALLORCA		
		No. (from N. to S.)		
	Technical Characteristics	Name	Municipality	Type of Management
1.	E	Port-Bou	Port-Bou	CPC
2.	E	Sant Miquel de Colera	Colera	CE
3.	E	Llançà	Llançà	CPC
4.	P	Port de la Selva	Port de la Selva	CPC
5.	P	Roses	Roses	CPC
6.	M	Sta. Margarida	Roses	CI
7.	M	Ampuriabrava	Castelló d'Empúries	CE
8.	P	l'Escala	l'Escala	CPC
9.	P	l'Estartit	Torroella de Montgrí	CPC
10.	E	Aiguablava	Bagur	CE
11.	E	Llafranc	Palafrugell	CE
12.	P	Palamós	Palamós	CPC
13.	M	Port d'Aro	Castell d'Aro	CE
14.	P	St. Feliu de Guíxols	St. Feliu de Guíxols	CPC
15.	E	Cala Canyelles	Lloret	CE

16.	P	Blanes	Blanes	CPC
17.	P	Arenys de Mar	Arenys de Mar	CPC
18.	PE	El Balís	St. Andreu Llavaneres	CE
19.	E	Premià de Mar	Premià de Mar	
20.	PE	Masnou	El Masnou	CE
21.	PA	Barcelona	Barcelona	CA
22.	P	Garraf	Sitges	CPC
23.	PE	Aiguadolç	Sitges	CE
24.	P	Vilanova	Vilanova i la Geltrú	CPC
25.	E	Segur de Calafell	Calafell	CE
26.	E	Comarruga	Comarruga	CE
27.	P	Tarragona	Tarragona	JOP
28.	E	Salou	Vilasseca-Salou	CE
29.	P	Cambrils	Cambrils	CPC
30.	E	Sant Jordi d'Alfama	L'Ametlla de Mar	CE
31.	P	Port pesquer de l'Ametlla	L'Ametlla de Mar	CPC
32.	E	L'Estany ras	L'Ametlla de Mar	CPC
33.	P	L'Ampolla	El Perelló	CPC
34.	P	St. Carles de la Ràpita	St. Carles de la Ràpita	CPC
35.	P	Cases d'Alcanar	Alcanar	CPC
36.		Palma de Mallorca	Palma de Mallorca	

E	Quay or Pier		CPC	Ports Commission of Catalunya
P	Port		CE	Sports Concession
M	Marina		CA	Board of Directors
PE	Pleasure Harbour		JOP	Port Authority
PA	Autonomous Port			

seamarks and shallow areas which may break the waves are not suitable and neither are those areas with very deep water close to the shore as the regatta triangle buoys cannot be anchored.

The main problem in using an existing marina would be that it would already be very occupied. If the Olympic sailing events were held in some of the existing ports many alterations would have to be carried out both to the buildings and the quays over sheltered waters. This work could cost less than building a new port but the quality, general design, services, and efficiency would not be as good. In Munich, Montreal, and Moscow it was decided to build a new port with all the basic facilities. If Barcelona also decided to do this, the construction of the facilities could be done by the Olympic Organization. The Organization could manage the complex during the Olympic Games and afterwards it could be signed over to any sports organization prepared to pay the cost of the work carried out. The opposite procedure could also be carried out, i.e. Give authorization for the building and management of the port to a private enterprise with the condition that it was not to be exploited until after the Games.

Volleyball

The features of a volleyball pavilion are almost identical to those for basketball and handball. The playing area must be 9 × 18 metres × 12 metres high but the whole competition area measures 20 × 34 metres. We propose to hold the finals in the Olympic Pavilion on Montjuïc. The preliminaries will be held in two new pavilions planned for the Valle Hebrón area and the Parc de Mar, in the Poble Nou area. As soon as these pavilions are opened they will be used at city level for the relevant districts.

Water polo

The finals of the water polo event are usually held in the swimming events pool, with seating for 10,000 spectators. The preliminary rounds can be held in a different pool with a playing area measuring

33×20 metres, with a seating capacity for about 4,000. We propose to use the Bernardo Picornell pools on Montjuïc for the preliminaries. The finals could be held in the same pool or in the Parc de Mar Olympic pool if this solution were more convenient.

Press Facilities

About 9,000 journalists, and radio and television technicians will need accomodation during the Games. A Press City could be built or the existing hotel accomodation could be used. In either case the accomodation should be located near the place of work, i.e. where the events are being held and near the Press Centre. Good transport and communications will be needed. The Press Centre will be the daily workplace for the journalists and their total space requirements will be around 18,000 to 21,000 m². In every set of facilities used for an Olympic event there will be an ancillary Press Centre, which will be well equipped and suited to information requirements of the events being covered.

It would not appear advisable to plan the construction of a Press City which would function as a separate quarter. There is enough hotel accomodation in Barcelona and the surrounding area to house the journalists comfortably.

We propose to locate the Press Centre in the present Congress Building inside the International Fair area on Montjuïc. This building has an area of over 20,000 m² and many different rooms and facilities. In addition to the ancillary Press Centres in each set of facilities where events are being held, there will also be general ancillary Press Centres in each Olympic area.

The Olympic Village

Accomodation for around 15,000 athletes and those accompanying them will be needed. Of this number 3,000 will be women. There are many different possibilities for this accomodation: individual apartments, studio apartments, 3 or 5 room flats, etc. The ratio of one type of accomodation to another will depend on the use to which these buildings will be put after the Games. The Olympic Village will be a single residential complex with separate accomodation for men and women. Suitable security measures will be necessary. As the Village will be an autonomous complex, there will be various complementary buildings.

The first option is to locate the Olympic Village in the Parc de Mar area on the land which will become available after the railway is buried underground together with land reclaimed from the sea by means of the beach and coastline protection operations. This action should be considered as one of urban renovation designed to solve some of the housing and general facility problems in the Poble Nou area. After the Olympic Games the 350,000 m² of accomodation, and the cultural, administrative, sports, shopping, recreational and social services facilities will be absorbed into the urban network.

The Olympic Village can be built through a public organization or a municipal foundation and later be sold or let. It would also be advisable to consider the participation of private companies or a mixture of private and public capital in the financing, construction, and selling of the dwellings. The facilities buildings should be publicly owned and be incorporated into the normal functioning of the city of Barcelona.

TABLE 6.

No.	Name	Sport	Ownership	Spectator Capacity	m² sports area	Paving etc.	New building	Remodelling	Improvements	83-86	87-89	90-92	TOTAL	LOCATION
	INSTALLATIONS FOR COMPETITIONS			CHARACTERISTICS			CONSTRUCTION COSTS			ESTIMATE OF INVESTMENTS				
1	Olympic Stadium	Athletics	PUB	55-60.000	22.000	Grass & art. turf	500	1.700	—	20	300	1.880	2.200	Montjuïc
2	20 kms Walk Course	Athletics	PUB	—	—	Asphalt	Included in development of the "Olympic Ring"						—	Montjuïc
3	20 kms Walk Course	Athletics	PUB	—	—	Asphalt	Included in development of the "Olympic Ring"						—	Montjuïc
4	42.195 km Marathon Course	Athletics	PUB	—	—	Asphalt	Included in basic road-works costs						—	Coastline
5	Serrahima Stadium	Athletics	PUB	1.500	14.850	Grass & art. turf	—	—	100	—	—	100	100	Montjuïc
6	"Julià de Capmany" Sp. Ground	Athletics	PUB	2.600	8.800	Grass	—	—	75	—	—	75	75	Montjuïc
7	"La Fuixarda" Rugby Ground	Athletics	PUB	1.100	8.700	Grass	—	—	40	—	—	40	40	Montjuïc
8	"Serrahima" Throwing Field	Athletics	PUB	—	7.000	Grass	—	—	20	—	—	20	20	Montjuïc
9	Olympic Sports Centre	Basketball	PUB	17.000	11.500	Parquet	3.800	—	—	3.100	—	700	3.800	Montjuïc
10	Blaugrana 1 Sports Centre	Basketball	PRI	5.244	970	Parquet	—	—	90	—	—	90	90	Diagonal
11	"Joventut de Badalona" Sp. Cent.	Basketball	PRI	4.500	800	Parquet	—	—	130	—	—	130	130	Coastline
12	Granollers Sports Centre	Handball	PUB	2.000	970	Parquet	—	—	150	—	—	150	150	—
13	Mataró Sports Centre	Handball	PUB	3.200	800	Parquet	—	—	150	—	—	150	150	Coastline
14	Barcelona Mncpl. Sports Centre	Boxing	PUB	7.500	1.500	Parquet	—	250	100	50	—	300	350	Montjuïc
15	"Valle Hebrón" Cycle Track	Cycling	PUB	7.500	250 m track inside	Wood	200	—	120	200	—	120	320	V. Hebrón
16	100 km Road Race Cycle Track	Cycling	PUB	—	Motorway 25 km x 4	Asphalt	Included in basic road-works costs						—	—
17	180 km Road Race	Cycling	PUB	—	Road 180 km	Asphalt	Included in basic road-works costs						—	—
18	Blaugrana Ice Rink	Fencing	PRI	3.000	1.600	—	—	—	90	—	—	90	90	Diagonal
19	"Camp Nou" Stad. F.C. Barcelona	Football	PRI	114.000	7.400	Grass	—	—	150	—	—	150	150	Diagonal
20	R.C.D. Español Stadium	Football	PRI	42.000	7.245	Grass	—	—	50	—	—	50	50	Diagonal
21	F.C. Barcelona "Mini-Stadium"	Football	PRI	15.300	6.700	Grass	—	—	20	—	—	20	20	Diagonal
22	"Creu Alta" Stadium. Sabadell	Football	PUB	20.000	6.695	Grass	—	—	50	—	—	50	50	Sabadell
23	Hospitalet Football Field	Football	PUB	10.000	5.850	Grass	—	—	50	—	—	50	50	Diagonal
24	"Renfe-Meridiana" Sports Centre	Weightlifting	PUB	3.000	970	Parquet	400	—	—	200	—	200	400	—
25	"Club de Polo" Riding Club	Equest.Sp.	PRI	10.000	242.000	Grass	150	50	150	50	50	250	350	Diagonal
26	Equestrian Run	Equest.Sp.	PUB	3.000	—	Earth	130	—	—	—	—	130	130	Montjuïc
27	"Pau Negre" Hockey Stadium	Hockey	PUB	7-10.000	6.000	Artificial Turf	300	—	—	150	—	150	300	Montjuïc
28	Terrassa Mncpl. Hockey Stadium	Hockey	PUB	7-10.000	6.000	Artificial Turf	—	150	100	70	30	150	250	Terrassa
29	Pla del Bonaire Hockey Field	Hockey	PRI	5-7.000	6.000	Artificial Turf	—	(100)	(100)	—	(50)	(150)	(200)	Terrassa
30	Hospitalet New Sports Centre	Judo	PUB	5-7.000	970	Parquet	400	—	—	200	—	200	400	Diagonal
31	"Mercat del Peix"	Wrestling	PUB	6-8.000	4.000	—	—	200	150	100	100	150	350	Poble Nou
32	"B. Picornell" Swimming Pools	Swimming	PUB	3-5.000	50x25/20x25 33 x 25	—	—	200	200	—	—	400	400	Montjuïc
33	"Parc de Mar" Swimming Pools	Swimming	PUB	10.000	50x25/20 x25 33 x 25	—	1.500	—	—	—	1.000	500	1.500	Poble Nou
34	"St. Jordi" Swimming Pool	Swimming	PUB	3-4.000	50 x 21	—	—	300	250	300		250	250	—
35a	"Mataro-Argentona" Shooting Range	Shooting	PUB	3-4.000	—	—	200	—	50	—	200	50	250	—
35b	"Parque Llobregat" Shooting Range	Shooting	PUB	3-4.000	—	—	(200)	—	(50)	—	(200)	(50)	(250)	Llobregat
36	Pentath. Course (4.000 m in dist.)	Pentathl.	PUB	—	—	Asphalt	Included in other installations and town-planning						—	Diagonal

TABLE 6.

No.	Name	Sport	Ownership	Spectator Capacity	m² sports area	Paving etc.	New building	Remodelling	Improvements	83-86	87-89	90-92	TOTAL	LOCATION
	INSTALLATIONS FOR COMPETITIONS			CHARACTERISTICS			CONSTRUCTION COSTS			ESTIMATE OF INVESTMENTS				
37a	Noguera-Pallaresa	Canoeing	PUB	15-20.000	—	—	—	—	70	—	—	70	70	—
37b	Envalira	Canoeing	PUB	15-20.000	—	—	—	—	(70)	—	—	(70)	(70)	—
37c	Garona	Canoeing	PUB	15-20.000	—	—	—	—	(70)	—	—	(70)	(70)	—
38a	Lake Banyoles	Rowing	PUB	10-12.000	—	—	250	—	250	150	100	250	500	—
38b	Llobregat Canal	Rowing	PUB	10-12.000	—	—	(4.300)	—	—	—	—	(4.300)	(4.300)	Llobregat
39	Barcelona Tennis	Tennis	PRI	10.000	14.400	Clay	—	—	50	—	—	50	50	Diagonal
40	R.C. Polo Tennis	Tennis	PRI	3.000	25.600	Clay	—	—	25	—	—	25	25	Diagonal
41	Turó Tennis	Tennis	PRI	3.000	14.400	Clay	—	—	25	—	—	25	25	Diagonal
42	"Palau Nacional"	Tab.Tennis	PUB	5.000	6.000	—	—	—	90	—	—	90	90	Montjuïc
43a	Diagonal Archery	Archery	PUB	3.000	—	Grass	—	—	180	—	—	180	180	Diagonal
43b	"Parque Llobregat" Archery	Archery	PUB	3.000	—	Grass	—	—	(180)	—	—	(180)	(180)	Llobregat
44	Pleasure Harbour	Sailing	PUB	—	—	—	4.000	—	—	—	2.000	2.000	4.000	—
45	"Parc de Mar" Sports Centre	Volleyball	PUB	5.000	3.500	Parquet	450	—	—	—	200	250	450	Poble Nou
46	"Parc Valle Hebrón" Sports Centre	Volleyball	PUB	5.000	3.500	Parquet	450	—	—	—	200	250	450	V. Hebrón
	TOTAL						12.730	2.850	2.975	4.590	4.180	9.785	18.555	
47	Montjuïc Press Sub-Centre	—	PUB	—	11.000 m² roof	—	550	—	—	550	—	550	550	Montjuïc
48	Diagonal Press Sub-Centre	—	PRI	—	10.000 m²	—	—	—	130	—	—	130	130	Diagonal
49	Poble Nou Press Sub-Centre	—	PUB	—	3.000	—	170	—	—	—	—	170	170	Poble Nou
50	Valle Hebrón Press Sub-Centre	—	PUB	—	1.500	—	90	—	—	—	—	90	90	V. Hebrón
51	Banyoles Press Sub-Centre	—	PUB	—	2.000	—	130	—	—	—	—	130	130	Banyoles
52	Pleasure Harbour Press Sub-Centre	—	PUB	—	2.500	—	150	—	—	—	—	150	150	Port
53	Llobregat Press Sub-Centre													
54	Palacio Congress Press Centre	—	PUB	—	22.000	—	—	—	300	—	—	300	300	Montjuïc
	TOTAL						1.090	—	430	—	550	970	1.520	
55	Olympic Village a) Poble Nou b) Vallés-Cerdanyola	—	PUB-PRI	—	400.000 m² roof	—	14.000	—	—	—	7.000	7.000	14.000	Poble Nou
56	Banyoles Olympic Village	—	PUB-PRI	—	12.000 m²	—	400	—	—	—	—	400	400	Banyoles
57	Harbour Olympic Village	—	PUB-PRI	—	35.000 m²	—	1.500	—	—	—	700	800	1.500	—
58a	Llobregat Youth Camp													
58b	University Youth Camp	—	PUB-PRI	—	—	—	300	—	—	—	—	300	300	Llobregat
58c	Tibidabo Youth Camp													
59	Judges & Referees' Residence		PUB	—	66.000	—	2.640	—	—	—	—	2.640	2.640	Val.-Cerd.
	TOTAL						18.840	—	—	—	7.700	11.140	18.840	

TABLE 6.

				CHARACTERISTICS			CONSTRUCTION COSTS			ESTIMATE OF INVESTMENTS				LOCATION
INSTALLATIONS FOR COMPETITIONS				Spectator Capacity	m² sports area	Paving etc.	New building	Remod- elling	Improve- ments	83-86	87-89	90-92	TOTAL	
No.	Name	Sport	Ownership											
101	C. N. Montjuïc	Athletics	PRI	—	6 lanes	Synthetic Ash	—	—	100	—	—	100	100	Montjuïc
102	F. C. Barcelona Athletics Track	Athletics	PRI	—	8 lanes	Synthetic	150	—	50	150	—	50	200	Diagonal
103	Olympic Village Athletics Track	Athletics	PUB	—	8 lanes	Synthetic	200	—	—	—	—	200	200	Poble Nou
104	Hospitalet Athletics Track	Athletics	PUB	—	8 lanes	Synthetic	150	—	50	150	—	50	200	Diagonal
105	Granollers Athletics Track	Athletics	PUB	2.000	8 lanes	Synthetic	—	—	80	—	—	80	80	—
106	Cornellà Athletics Track	Athletics	PUB	1.500	6 lanes	Synthetic	—	—	80	—	—	80	80	Llobregat
107	St. Josep. Badalona	Basketball	PUB	1.600	700	Parquet	—	—	90	—	—	90	90	Coastline
108	"La Salle". Bonanova/Barcelona	Basketball	PRI	800	800	Synthetic	—	—	90	—	—	90	90	Foothills
109	AES. Sarriá/Barcelona	Basketball	PRI	500	800	Parquet	—	—	90	—	—	90	90	Foothills
110	Blaugrana-2. Barcelona	Basketball	PRI	5.244	970	Cement	—	—	90	—	—	90	90	Diagonal
111	INEF. Esplugues	Basketball	PUB	300	1.230	Synthetic	—	—	90	—	—	90	90	Diagonal
112	España Industrial Pavilion	Handball	PUB	—	1.200	Synthetic	350	—	—	100	200	50	350	—
113	"Barcelona Squash"	Handball	PRI	—	800	Synthetic	—	—	50	—	—	50	50	Diagonal
114	"Llars Mundet"	Handball	PUB	500	1.075	Parquet	—	—	90	—	—	90	90	V. Hebrón
115	University Sports Grounds	Handball	PUB	—	1.200	Synthetic	—	—	90	—	—	90	90	Diagonal
116	"Unió Esportiva Horta"	Boxing	PUB	1.000	800	—	—	—	40	—	—	40	40	V. Hebrón
117	"Can Vidalet". Esplugues	Boxing	PUB	500	800	—	—	—	40	—	—	40	40	Llobregat
118	St. Just Desvern Pavilion	Boxing	PUB	1.000	968	—	—	—	40	—	—	40	40	Llobregat
119	Hospitalet Pavilion	Boxing	PUB	1.800	800	—	—	—	40	—	—	40	40	Diagonal
120	Alfonso XIII Sports Centre. Bclna.	Fencing	PUB			—	—	—	85	—	—	85	85	Montjuïc
121	St. Andreu Football Grounds	Football	PUB	—			—	—	50	—	—	50	50	—
122	St. Boi Football Grounds	Football	PUB	—			—	—	50	—	—	50	50	Llobregat
123	Camp Nou 2. Masia Barça Bclna.	Football	PRI	—		Grass	—	—	50	—	—	50	50	Diagonal
124	Granollers Football Stadium	Football	PUB	3.500			—	—	50	—	—	50	50	—
125	Terrassa Football Stadium	Football	PUB	17.000			—	—	50	—	—	50	50	—
126	"La Fuixarda" Gymnasium	Gymnastics	PUB	1.000	1.000	—	50	20	70	70	—	70	140	Montjuïc
127	Olympic Sports Centre Training	Gymnastics	PUB	—			Included in the Olympic Sports Centre costs							Montjuïc
128	"Parq. Valle Hebrón" Gymnasium	Gymnastics	PUB	—			300	—	—	100	100	100	300	V. Hebrón
129	St. Feliu Llobregat Sports Centre	Gymnastics	PUB	1.008			150	—	90	150	—	90	240	Llobregat
130	Victoria Eugenia Sports Centre	Weightlifting	PUB	—			—	—	85	—	—	85	85	Montjuïc
131	Equestrian Circuits	Eque. Spor.	PUB	—			80	—	—	—	—	80	80	Diagonal
132	R.C. Polo Hockey Field	Hockey	PRI	18.000		Artificial Turf	—	120	—	—	120	—	120	Diagonal
133	St. Cugat "Junior"	Hockey	PRI	—		Artificial Turf	—	120	—	—	120	—	120	—
134	Metallurgy Pavilion. Barcelona	Judo	PUB	—	9.900	—	—	—	80	—	—	80	80	Montjuïc
135	Pavilion No. 1. Barcelona	Wrestling	PUB	—	9.900	—	—	—	100	—	—	100	100	Montjuïc
136	Sabadell Swimming Club	Swimming Diving	PUB	2.000	—	—	—	—	40	—	—	40	40	—
137	Mataró Swimming Club	Swimming Diving	PRI	1.500	—	—	—	—	130	—	—	130	130	Coastline
138	Granollers Swimming Club	Swimming Diving	PUB	1.500	—	—	—	—	130	—	—	130	130	—
139	Montjuïc Swimming Club	Swimming	PRI	—	—	—	—	—	40	—	—	40	40	Montjuïc
140	"Llars Mundet"	Relay Swimming	PUB	—	—	—	—	—	40	—	—	40	40	V. Hebrón
141	Guinardó. Barcelona	Relay Swimming	PUB	—	—	—	—	—	40	—	—	40	40	V. Hebrón

TABLE 6.

INSTALLATIONS FOR COMPETITIONS				CHARACTERISTICS			CONSTRUCTION COSTS			ESTIMATE OF INVESTMENTS				LOCATION
No.	Name	Sport	Ownership	Spectator Capacity	m² sports area	Paving etc.	New building	Remod- elling	Improve- ments	83-86	87-89	90-92	TOTAL	
142	Mequinenza Reservoir	Rowing Canoeing Kayaking	PUB	—	—	—	80	—	—	—	—	80	80	—
143	Montjuïc Shooting Range	Shooting	PUB	—	—	—	—	80	50	—	100	30	130	Montjuïc
144	"La Caixa" Pavilion. Barcelona	Volleyball	PRI	200	800	Parquet	—	—	50	—	—	50	50	Foothills
145	"Hispano Francés"	Volleyball	PRI	1.200	800	Parquet	—	—	50	—	—	50	50	V. Hebron
146	Vallés-Cerdanyola Training Zone						350	—	—	—	150	200	350	—
	TOTAL						1.860	340	2.530	720	790	3.220	4.730	—

52

Cost of the installations

Table 6 shows all the training and event facilities and installations for the Olympic Games and specifies for which sport they will be used, whether the facilities are publicly or privately owned, their main features, and the costs for construction, renovation or improvement and preparation estimated for each. The following columns list the forecasts for investment during the 1983-1986, 1987-1989, and 1990-1992 periods, the total cost of the installation and the area in which it is situated.

The amounts shown in brackets in the table correspond to alternative solutions or variations. These are not featured in the total sum but give an idea of the increase or reduction in costs involved if the solution chosen were to be varied. The total cost of the event installations and facilities is 18,555 million while the training facilities will cost 4,730 million. The costs for those installations mentioned in previous chapters as other training facilities have not been calculated as they are auxiliary or to replace other installations. In any case the improvements to these facilities are restricted to the normal investments of their public or private ownership.

1

2

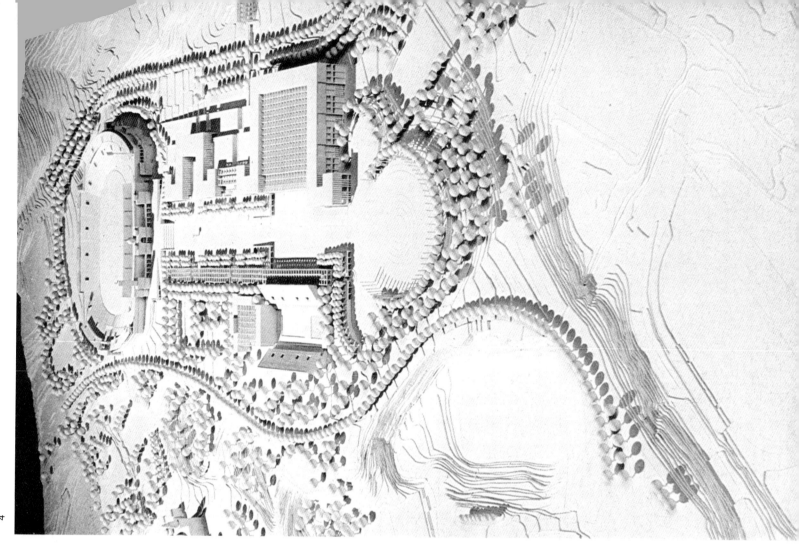

4

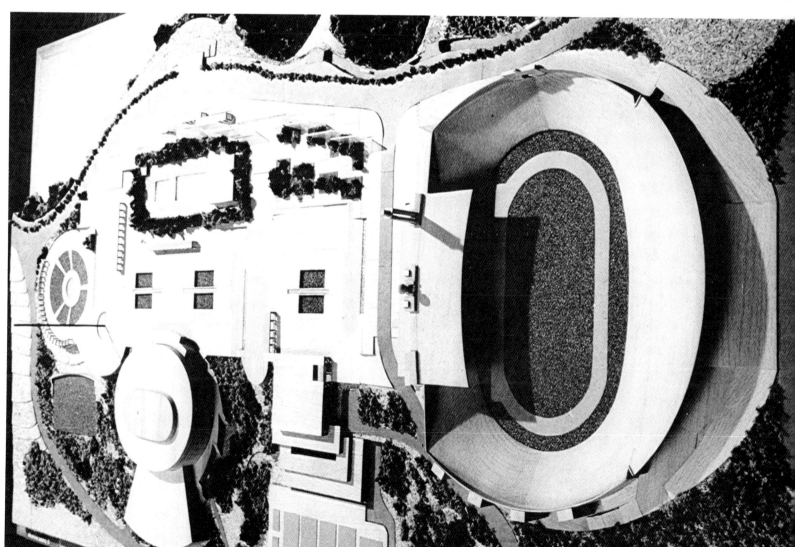

3

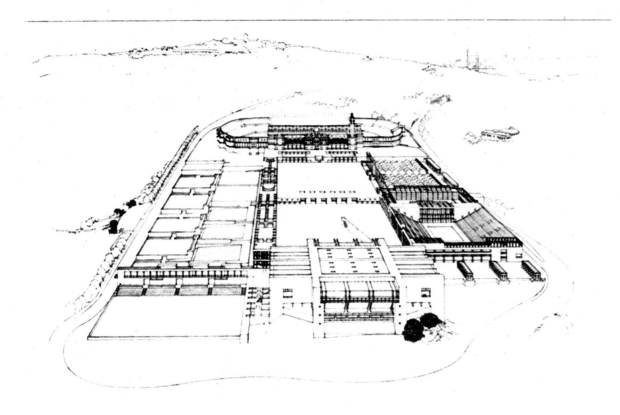

11

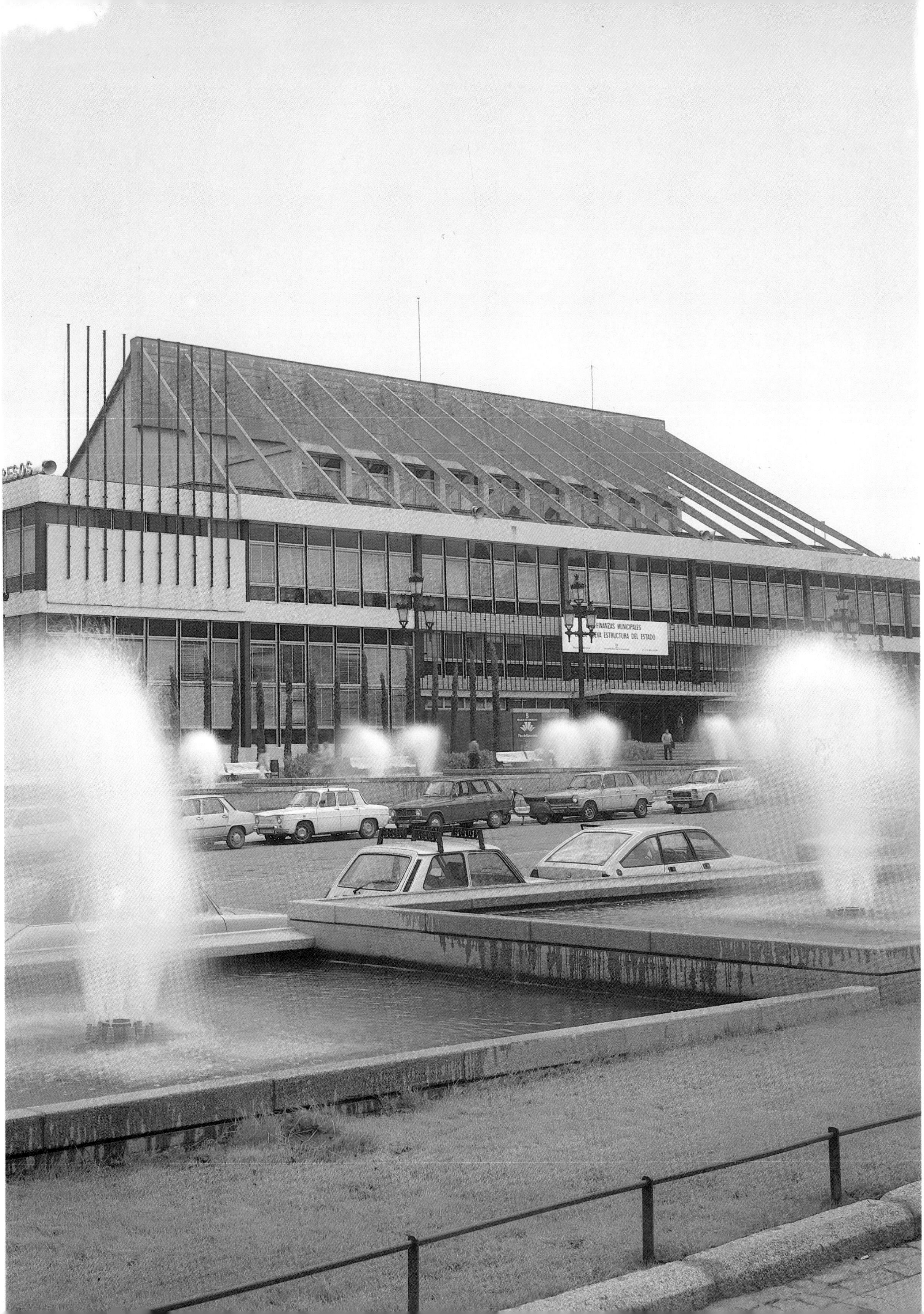

16

17

21

22

25

23

24

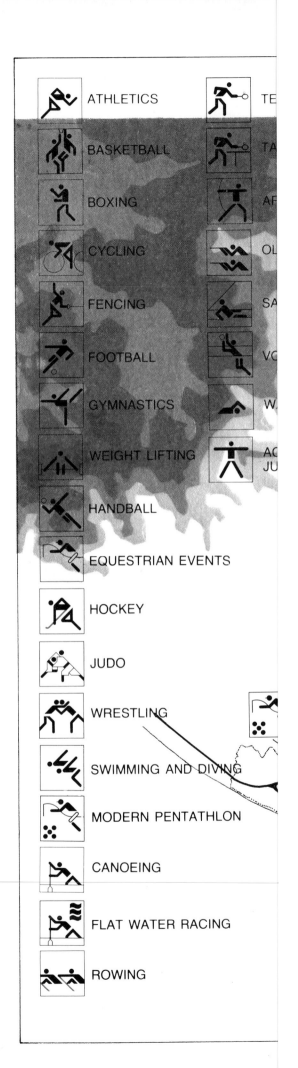

ATHLETICS

TE

BASKETBALL

TA

BOXING

AF

CYCLING

OL

FENCING

SA

FOOTBALL

VC

GYMNASTICS

W

WEIGHT LIFTING

AC
JU

HANDBALL

EQUESTRIAN EVENTS

HOCKEY

JUDO

WRESTLING

SWIMMING AND DIVING

MODERN PENTATHLON

CANOEING

FLAT WATER RACING

ROWING

INDEX OF PHOTOGRAPHS

The international tender for the construction of the facilities complex known as the "Olympic Ring" (remodelling of the Stadium to take up to 70,000 spectators; reshaping of the "Bernat Picornell" swimming pools; and the construction of the Sports Pavilion – 17,000 spectators – and the Ancillary Press Centre, the future Physical Education Centre, had excellent results.

ORGANIZATION

The *organization* of an important event is generally understood to consist of planned actions interwoven together and channelled towards their ultimate and appropriate completion. The present study of the organization of the Olympic Games is thus aimed at determining what the necessary materials and human resources for its preparation and running will be and how they will be set up. The scope of this study is focused mainly on the *management of resources* rather than the means of obtaining them. This point is considered in greater detail in the study of the Olympic installations which explains how these basic resources –the installations and financing– for the proper functioning of the Olympic Games will be provided.

Main conclusions

Meeting the legal requirements. According to the Olympic Charter, the honour of holding the Olympic Games is entrusted to a city. The intervention of central governments depends on the internal structure adopted in each case; nevertheless, the official authority of the city concerned normally undertakes the responsibility of the Games.

The rights of a municipality organizing the Olympiad are clearly legitimate. There are no legal obstacles standing in the way of the aspirations of the Town Hall of Barcelona in this respect.

Upon having examined the Rules, Bye-Laws and Instructions of the Olympic Charter, no substantial contradiction whatever with Spanish laws can be observed; on the contrary, these above-mentioned Rules, Bye-Laws and Instructions are intended to achieve the best organization possible of the Olympic Games under standards of conduct which would be unachievable if each country in which the Games are held were to prepare its own rules. This objective is congruent with the provisions of article 43.3. of the Spanish Constitution, which obliges the government bodies to foster sports, of which the Olympics are evidently the maximum expression.

Meeting the organizational requirements. In spite of the importance and complexity inherent in the organization of an Olympiad, we can fully affirm after the studies carried out that Barcelona, Catalunya and Spain possess in every respect the organizational ability necessary to hold the XXV Olympic Games in 1992.

Indeed, both human resources and the required standard of services have already been put to the test in international competitions of high standing with the recent World Cup of Football as an outstanding example. The next major events to be held in Spain (World Championships of Cycling, Gymnastics, Swimming and Basketball) should further consolidate this experience and also project our organizing capability to the world.

Human resources.

Table 7

	HEADING	1987	1988	1989	1990	1991	JFM 1992	AM 1992	JJ 1992	ASOND 1992	1993
1	ADMINISTRATION										
1.1	Personnel Admnstrtn.	1	2	2	3	3	4	5	8	3	1
1.2	Part time pers. selec./train.	0	0	0	0	0	2	2	2	0	0
1.3	Administrative centre	8	12	18	30	60	60	60	60	18	18
1.4	Accounting	3	5	7	10	15	15	15	15	10	5
1.5	Legal services	1	2	2	4	4	4	4	4	2	1
1.6	Finance	8	8	16	16	16	20	20	20	16	8
1.7	Purchases & storage	2	3	7	18	45	90	90	90	25	7
1.8	General services	2	5	8	10	25	25	25	25	10	4
1.9	Insurances										
1.10	Premises	1	1	1	2	3	4	16	16	2	1
1.11	General expenditures										
1.12	Auditing	1	1	2	3	5	15	15	15	4	1
1.13	Cleaning	27	39	63	96	176	239	252	255	90	46
2	TECHNOLOGY										
2.1	Data processing	2	2	3	5	5	10	50	450	20	2
2.2	Radio & television	2	2	3	5	5	10	10	10	0	0
2.3	Telecommunications	2	2	2	3	3	5	5	5	0	0
2.4	Scoreboards										
2.5	Track instruments										
	TECHNOLOGY TOTAL	6	6	8	13	13	25	65	465	20	2
3	SERVICES										
3.1	Protocol	1	1	4	2	3	10	20	30	1	0
3.2	Public relations	2	2	2	5	13	27	39	295	1	0
3.3	Hostesses & guides	0	1	2	2	6	200	400	1,200	0	0
3.4	Language services	1	2	4	10	10	50	100	150	4	4
3.5	Health & med. cntrl.	1	1	3	6	10	10	10	160	0	0
3.6	Traffic control	0	1	1	1	2	2	5	5	0	0
3.7	Transports	1	1	1	2	7	30	50	3,300	8	3
3.8	Lodgings admnstrtn.	0	0	0	2	10	25	50	50	0	0
3.9	Ticket admnstrtn.										
	SERCICES TOTAL	6	9	14	30	61	354	674	5,190	14	7
4	PRESS & PBLCTN. TOTAL										
4.1	Press cabinet	2	2	2	3	5	10	15	25	4	1
4.2	Archives & documents	2	2	3	3	3	5	10	10	10	1
4.3	Publications	2	4	4	5	15	25	25	95	4	2
4.4	Press centres	0	0	0	0	2	3	10	1,700	0	0
	PRESS & PUBLICAT. TOTAL	6	8	9	11	25	43	60	1,830	18	4
5	IMAGE										
5.1	Designs & graphics	2	5	10	10	18	18	18	18	0	0
5.2	Publicity/promotion	1	3	5	5	5	5	5	5	0	0
	IMAGE TOTAL	3	8	15	15	23	23	23	23	0	0
6	TOWN PLANNING										
6.1	Town planning	8	8	16	16	20	20	20	20	2	0
	TOTAL TOWN PLANNING	8	8	16	16	20	20	20	20	2	0

7	**SECURITY**										
7.1	Security systems	0	0	0	0	0	0	0	14,000	0	0
7.2	Credentials	0	0	0	10	50	150	200	200	0	0
7.3	Public protection	0	0	0	0	2	2	2	2	0	0
7.4	COJO security	5	5	5	9	14	26	48	50	2	2
	SECURITY TOTAL	5	5	5	19	66	178	250	14,252	2	2
8	**OLYMPIC VILLAGE**										
8.1	COJO personnel	2	5	8	15	25	25	25	25	5	0
8.2	O. Village personnel	0	0	0	0	0	0	100	3,000	0	0
8.3	Meals										
8.4	Furnishings										
8.5	Maintenance										
8.6	Rent										
8.7	Olympic radio	0	0	0	0	0	2	10	40	0	0
	OLYMPIC VILLAGE TOTAL	2	5	8	15	25	27	135	3,065	5	0
9	**SPORTS**										
9.1	COJO personnel	2	15	25	80	100	125	125	125	0	0
9.2	Foreign judges & refs.	0	0	0	0	0	0	0	1,200	0	0
9.3	Spanish judges & refs.	0	0	0	0	0	0	0	1,500	0	0
9.4	Competition assistants	0	0	0	0	0	0	0	4,000	0	0
9.5	Buildings personnel	0	0	0	0	0	0	0	7,000	0	0
9.6	Training										
9.7	Equipment										
	SPORTS TOTAL	2	15	25	80	100	125	125	13,825	0	0
10	**CEREMONIES**										
10.1	COJO personnel	2	2	2	10	30	50	100	100	0	0
10.2	Olympic torch										
10.3	Inauguration	0	0	0	0	0	0	0	1,000	0	0
10.4	Medals										
10.5	Closure										
10.6	Congresses										
10.7	Flags										
	CEREMONIES TOTAL	2	2	2	10	30	50	100	1,100	0	0
11	**CULTURAL ACTIVITIES**										
11.1	Cultural activities	2	2	10	10	20	20	30	60	0	0
	CULTURALACTIVITIESTOTAL	2	2	10	10	20	20	30	60	0	0
12	**YOUTH CAMPS**										
12.1	Youth camps	0	0	0	2	3	3	12	300	0	0
	YOUTH CAMPS TOTAL	0	0	0	2	3	3	12	300	0	0
	TOTAL	69	107	175	317	562	1,107	1,746	40,385	151	61

C

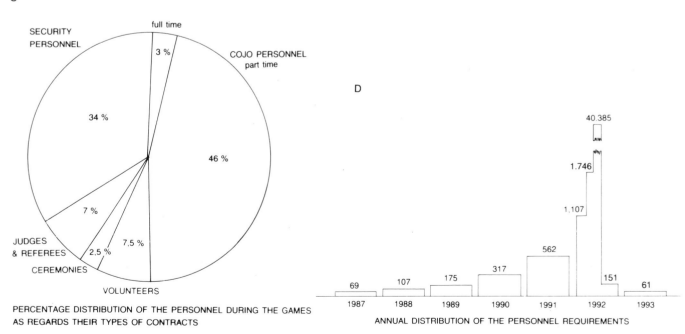

PERCENTAGE DISTRIBUTION OF THE PERSONNEL DURING THE GAMES
AS REGARDS THEIR TYPES OF CONTRACTS

ANNUAL DISTRIBUTION OF THE PERSONNEL REQUIREMENTS

E

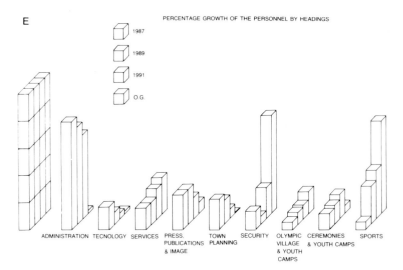

1987
1989
1991
O.G.

ADMINISTRATION TECNOLOGY SERVICES PRESS, PUBLICATIONS & IMAGE TOWN PLANNING SECURITY OLYMPIC VILLAGE & YOUTH CAMPS CEREMONIES & YOUTH CAMPS SPORTS

Table 8

Heading	Expenditures					Pos. Vol.	Total	Ceded goods
	Person.	Servi.	Equip.	Invest.	SUB.			
1 ADMINISTRATION								
1.1 Personnel Admnstrtn.	45	287	310	0	642		642	150
1.2 Part time pers. selec./training	3	182	63	0	248		248	0
1.3 Administrative centre	520	0	0	0	520		520	0
1.4 Accounting	160	0	0	0	160		160	0
1.5 Legal services	47	30	0	0	77		77	0
1.6 Finance	249	0	0	0	249		249	0
1.7 Purchases & storage	400	43	0	0	443		443	0
1.8 General services	201	0	0	0	201		201	0
1.9 Insurances	0	1,000	0	0	1,000		1,000	0
1.10 Premises	45	179	17	600	841		841	0
1.11 General expenditures	0	745	372	125	1,242		1,242	150
1.12 Auditing	65	50	0	0	115		115	0
1.13 Cleaning	0	64	13	0	77		77	0
ADMINISTRATION CONTROL	1,735	2,580	775	725	5,815	0	5,815	300
2 TECHNOLOGY								
2.1 Data processing	312	429	382	2,921	4,044		4,044	975
2.2 Radio & television	63	2,500	2,000	5,000	9,563		9,563	0
2.3 Telecommunications	41	0	1,500	150	1,691		1,691	50
2.4 Scoreboards	0	0	0	500	500		500	250
2.5 Track instruments	0	0	0	100	100		100	25
TECHNOLOGY TOTAL	416	2,929	3,882	8,671	15,898	0	15,898	1,300
3 SERVICES								
3.1 Protocol	53	631	42	0	726		726	0
3.2 Public relations	240	0	0	0	240		240	0
3.3 Hostesses & guides	904	0	0	0	904	153	751	0
3.4 Language services	240	0	20	0	260		260	0
3.5 Health & med. cntrl.	111	30	0	355	496		496	0
3.6 Traffic control	20	0	15	105	140		140	0
3.7 Transports	853	339	0	10	1,202	76	1,126	0
3.8 Lodgings admnstrtn.	96	0	0	0	96		96	0
3.9 Ticket admnstrtnn.	2,517	1,300	77	470	4,364	229	4,135	0
SERVICES TOTAL	2,517	1,300	77	470	4,364	229	4,135	0
4 PRESS & PUBLICATIONS								
4.1 Press cabinet	71	0	0	0	71		71	0
4.2 Archives & documents	63	0	0	0	63		63	0
4.3 Publications	165	0	914	0	1,079		1,079	0
4.4 Press centres	599	0	170	0	769		769	0
PRESS & PUBLICATIONS TOTAL	898	0	1,084	0	1,982	0	1,982	0
5 IMAGE								
5.1 Designs & graphics	153	250	280	0	683		683	0
5.2 Publicity/promotion	60	3,000	50	0	3,110	0	3,793	0
IMAGE TOTAL	213	3,250	330	0	3,793	0	3,793	0
6 TOWN PLANNING								
6.1 Town planning	222	0	0	0	222		222	0
TOTAL TOWN PLANNING	222	0	0	0	222	0	222	0

	(1)	(2)	(3)	(4)	SUB T.		TOTAL	
7 SECURITY								
7.1 Security systems	0	572	35	0	607		607	0
7.2 Credentials	453	15	100	0	568		568	0
7.3 Public protection	9	37	0	63	109		109	0
7.4 COJO security	176	0	0	50	226		226	0
SECURITY TOTAL	638	624	135	113	1,510	0	1,510	0
8 OLYMPIC VILLAGE								
8.1 COJO personnel	198	0	0	0	198		198	0
8.2 O. Village personnel	736	0	0	0	736		736	0
8.3 Meals	0	0	300	0	300		300	0
8.4 Furnishings	0	0	0	1,200	1,200		1,200	0
8.5 Maintenance	0	0	150	0	150		150	0
8.6 Rent	0	1,000	200	0	1,200		1,200	0
8.7 Olympic radio	24	0	0	12	36		36	0
OLYMPIC VILLAGE TOTAL	958	1,000	650	1,212	3,820	0	3,820	0
9 SPORTS								
9.1 COJO personnel	814	0	0	0	814		814	0
9.2 Foreign judges & refs.	0	312	0	0	312		312	0
9.3 Spanish judges & refs.	0	360	0	0	360		3600	
9.4 Competition assistants	690	0	0	0	690	173	517	0
9.5 Buildings personnel	1,208	0	0	0	1,208	173	1,035	0
9.6 Training	0	12	0	0	12		12	0
9.7 Equipment	0	0	100	0	100		100	0
SPORTS TOTAL	2,712	684	100	0	3,496	346	3,150	0
10 CEREMONIES								
10.1 COJO personnel	254	0	0	0	254		254	0
10.2 Olympic torch	0	50	10	0	60		60	0
10.3 Inauguration	0	200	0	0	200		200	0
10.4 Medals	0	0	14	0	14		14	0
10.5 Closure	0	150	0	0	150		150	0
10.6 Congresses	0	258	0	0	258		258	0
10.7 Flags	0	0	100	0	100		100	0
CEREMONIES TOTAL	254	658	124	0	1,036	0	1,036	0
11 CULTURAL ACTIVITIES								
11.1 Cultural activities	177	920	0	0	1,097		1,097	0
CULTURAL ACTIVITIES TOTAL	177	920	0	0	1,097	0	1,097	0
12 YOUTH CAMPS								
12.1 Youth camps	91	25	30	40	186		186	0
YOUTH CAMPS TOTAL	91	25	30	40	186	0	186	0
TOTAL	10,831	13,970	7,187	11,231	43,219	575	42,644	1,600

SUB T.: Sub total of the 4 previous columns.
TOTAL: Net expenditure.

This is a breakdown under the headings which make for a detailed study of the personnel requirements of each one of the twelve areas taken into consideration. As can be observed, from the seventy people needed in the first year, the presence of more than forty thousand is reached during the time when the Games are to be held.

In order to fathom the magnitude which the holding of the Olympic Festival represents, we might underline that the total manhours needed works out at 3.924 man years.

The organizing costs. Table 8 has the same headings breakdown as table n.° 7 and presents a résumé of the estimate of the organizing costs of the Games. The personnel costs are presented without taking the possibility of volunteers into consideration. That is why the reduced figures of these costs have been indicated: in case the volunteers, estimated at three thousand, can be found.

In addition, the estimated value of the materials obtained through cessions, which thus do not entail any cost, have been included as a reference point. As can be seen, the total running costs are estimated at 42.644 million pesetas of which twenty-four per cent is earmarked to personnel costs, thirty-three per cent to contracting services, seventeen per cent to the purchase of materials and the remaining twenty-six per cent is assigned to investments. Since this estimate of expenses has been divided into years, it is possible to show an annual distribution of the running costs. It can be seen that sixty-four per cent of the expenses occur the year in which the Games are held; a further eighteen per cent takes place in both the year prior to the Games as well as in the four-year-period of 1987-1990. The expenses incurred during the year of liquidation of the Organizing Committee (COJO) are minimal.

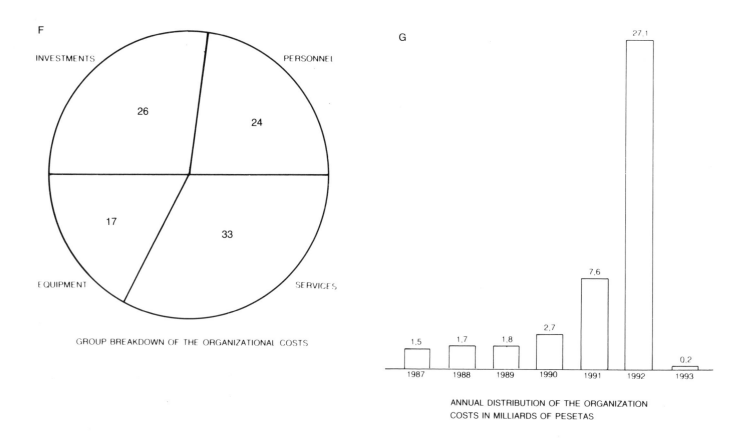

F

INVESTMENTS

PERSONNEL

26

24

17

33

EQUIPMENT

SERVICES

GROUP BREAKDOWN OF THE ORGANIZATIONAL COSTS

G

27,1

7,6

1,5   1,7   1,8   2,7

0,2

1987   1988   1989   1990   1991   1992   1993

ANNUAL DISTRIBUTION OF THE ORGANIZATION
COSTS IN MILLIARDS OF PESETAS

Preparation of the candidature: The phase that is covered in the preparation and presentation of this: preliminary plan is the threshold of a period of hard work, the main purpose of which is obtaining the nomination of Barcelona as the XXV Olympiad headquarters.

The main task of the next phase will consist of drafting a candidature project. Although the greater part of the preparations for the Games need not begin until after the designation of the Olympic city, some of it will needfully have to be started beforehand. To this effect, emphasis should be given to the activities related to data processing services, radio, television, telecommunications and housing.

As regards the data processing services, it will be necessary to encourage investigation in up-to-date technologies which might present an opportunity for the Spanish electronics sector. With reference to radio, television and telecommunications, all new products and services should be followed and evaluated. With regards to lodging, it would be advisable to give incentives to the building of more first-class hotels as well as refurbishing those already in existence. A convention centre should also be built and the universities could be endowed with new halls of residency.

Hypotheses used

The *estimations base*: The prices of 1983 were used to estimate expenditures. Inflationary effects have not been included.

Personnel expenditures: The average gross salary for contracted personnel is estimated at two million pesetas. To this figure we must add approximately thirty per cent as social security and benefits as well as about eight per cent as severance pay. The total average annual cost of a COJO employee can thus be estimated at 2,760,000 pesetas.

The cession of materials: It can be imagined that the manufacturers of certain materials necessary for the running of the Games will freely transfer some of their products to the COJO during a limited time. The value of these goods (office and data-processing equipment, radio transmitters, etc.) has not been entered in the books as an expenditure. The total value of these loans has been estimated at approximately 1,600 million pesetas, which represents eight per cent of the anticipated total purchases and investments.

Reinvestment of the investments: Apart from those goods which are to be ceded to the COJO, the necessary goods and equipment will be purchased. Nevertheless, the greater part of the property and goods to be purchased which can be considered as investments are also subject to reuse and will thus entail a minimal outlay.

The estimate of expenditures does not foresee this situation and all the purchase prices of these materials are represented in whole. In the estimate of income this, the partial recovery of some of the expenditures by reselling the assets of the COJO during its winding up, has in fact been taken into consideration.

Considered sports programme: Throughout this organizational study we have reckoned that the sports programme for the XXVth Olympiad should be same twenty-three planned for Seoul in 1988. Two other additional sports will also be exhibited.

Participants: In terms of the expectives of the Los Angeles Olympic Games (9,600 athletes with 4,000 back-up personnel), we have estimated that the total amount of athletes and technical advisers in the 1992 Games will rise to approximately 15,000 people. In terms of the sports considered and the increase in the number of athletes, there will be a need for around 2,700 judges and referees. The Olympic Charter currently provides for the concession of 7,800 accreditation cards for mass-media personnel at the Summer Games. Due to the continual increases that have occured in previous Olympics, we are expecting approximately 9,000 in 1992.

Dates for holding the Olympic Games: It is still too early to pinpoint the exact dates on which the Games would be held. In order to make this decision, it will be necessary to consult the indices of rainfall and other meteorological statistics as well as evaluating the advantages and disadvantages which one or another date might present. A preliminary approximation to this would then indicate that the Games could possibly be inaugurated on June 27th and brought to a close on July 12th.

The proposed organization

*A*dministration. The organization of the Olympic Games demands efficient and reliable methods. In effect it is necessary to set up an extremely eventful enterprise in a short time and for a short time. The administrative work will be abundant and varied: selecting, hiring, accrediting and remunerating personnel; controlling the budget; obtaining supplies, insurance and legal services; maintaining and providing security for the buildings and premises, and so forth.

Uniforms: It is necessary to show the world an image of elegance and common sense in dress whenever running an event that is as widely-broadcast as are the Olympic Games. It is therefore important to design uniforms which show the duties of the COJO employees as well as adding a touch of extra colour. With this goal in mind, the Grupo de Diseño Barcelona-92, in operation since April 1984, will play a decisive role in not only the designing of uniforms but also in everything that refers to the Games and which might affect the image of Barcelona-92.

Data processing: In this day and age of telecommunications and computer technology, the visitors and employees of the 1992 Olympics will expect the services of security, management and information to be extensive, safe, reliable and, above all, friendly. The information services network is to spread out over fifty sports grounds and press centres as well as providing information to the public at large and about ticket booths, hotels and private residences. All of these interrelated factors taken together form, due to their magnitude, a veritable information processing Olympiad that is as highly significant for Spain culturally, commercially, industrially, technologically, and scientifically as the strictly sports event is for sports and culture.

Computers will be an indispensable tool for the preparation and carrying out of the Olympic Games. An organizational success depends largely on the computers operating smoothly. The different systems to be used must therefore meet strict requirements of integrity and security. Access to the information banks must be restricted in order to guarantee confidentiality and prevent frauds. The data processing systems must be totally trustworthy in order to inspire absolute confidence in the information. The installations will have security controls against sabotage or accidents. There will be uninterrupted availability in order to assure a complete service without any delays. Data processers are considered a back-up *de rigueur* in the Olympic organization as regards the sports events (regulating registrations and results), as regards the COJO (accounting and other parts of business management) and as regards the mass media (information on enrolments, events and results). But the organizing committee needs an absolutely reliable system which guarantees the same security for everybody. It also has obligations with regard to the public not participating in the competitions. Therefore, apart from the essential ones, it would be advisable to install other programs and systems to aid in the preparation and control of plans and projects, accreditations, lodgings administration, reserving and selling tickets, medical administration, link-ups with press agencies and the major data bank networks, word processing, classifying messages, controling technical systems, security and so forth.

Radio and Television

The state of radio and television in Barcelona: Being in an area with a great amount of AM and FM radio stations – the latter have grown on a large scale in recent years – Barcelona and its outskirts compose an extremely rich radiocommunications spectrum. If we consider Barcelona's zone of influence as being all Catalunya, then we come across the presence of RNE and RCE, the two state-owned broadcasting stations; Catalunya Radio, another government controlled station covering Catalunya; in the same way, there are several large private networks such as SER, COPE, RCC, Antena-3, Radio-80 and Cadena-13. There is also an important number of local broadcasting stations which have remained independent of the large networks; it is quite interesting to point out that amongst these local stations there are a great many municipally-owned ones which by themselves have a lot of potential. These occasionally emit programmes together, forming a minor network.

Barcelona is the second television centre in Spain as regards total production. On the one hand, there is the production centre in Sant Cugat del Vallés which has just completed its first phase of construction. This first phase includes several services such as two continuity studios and two production studios. When the project reaches its end, it will count with six production and two continuity studios.

On the other hand, TV-3 – the autonomous government's channel in Catalunya – is currently making use of provisional studios as its permanent ones are under construction in Sant Joan Despí. TV-3 will have installations and production capacity similar to TVE when completed.

Moreover, Barcelona, due to its special geographical location, is the signal input and output station for the UER network through which signals originating in Europe are relayed through Spain to Africa and vice-versa.

Availability of resources: Starting with the means presently available and the foreseen modernization and increase of these in the near future, and taking into account the vast importance that television plays in the Olympics and the significance of the technical requirements, we shall now put forward a hypothetical exploitation of the present resources and how they would meet the above-mentioned technical requirements of television. We are not mentioning the resources and requirements of radio here as this medium has substantially lower costs than television as well as a very different impact.

The precise infrastructure for the unilaterals: TVE studios in Sant Cugat del Vallés, TV-3 studios in Sant Joan Despí and the RTV Olympic Games Centre which is to be located in the tradefair grounds on Montjuïc.

Linkage capacity: the new tower on Tibidabo which, due to its location, will surely be able to directly cover, without intermediaries, the greater part of the Olympic emplacements. The use of satellites to broadcast the signals and act as relay stations is a point to be considered in the next eight years.

Capacity to cover the live broadcasts: a large reserve of mobile units will have to be available owing to the many Olympic activities and their different emplacements. The following possibilities have been considered as ways to attend to these needs: 1) modernizing and revamping the mobile units purchased for the 1982 World Cup of Football; 2) using the mobile units which belong to the autonomous governments' channels; 3) adquiring mobile units specially for the 1992 Games; 4) mobile units provided by other European nations, either as loans or special agreements for this event.

An organization capable of administrating these materials and meeting the needs of the radio and television stations broadcasting the event should be created. This agency, which we have called the "Organismo de Radio Televisión de los Juegos Olímpicos (ORTJO)", is to supply the images and audio for international live broadcasting to the Spanish and foreign radio and television accredited by the COJO for that purpose.

The five goals of the ORTJO will be: 1) guaranteeing the televised and filmed coverage of the Games by supplying the images and audio from each point of competition; 2) setting up the necessary installations in each point of competition for the live transmission of radio and television commentaries. 3) setting up a fully equipped broadcasting centre complete with all the necessary means for each stage of production and transmission; 4) providing the necessary television and radio services and installations so that the broadcasters can produce their own transmissions; 5) guaranteeing the transmission of the different national stations, according to the criteria of the broadcasters.

Services: The Organizing Committee has committed itself to properly looking after the members of the Olympic family and the visitors during their stay in the Olympic city. With this purpose in mind we have made studies of all the services which will make the stay of the Olympic family more enjoyable. Thus, we have already given consideration to topics such as protocol, receptions, public relations, congress hostesses, tour guides, interpretation services, sanitation, medical services, air traffic control, transportation, accommodation and ticket distribution and control.

Before going on to analysing the final points in this section on Organization, we would like to point out that the Board of Directors of the candidature of Barcelona-92 have already prepared very complete studies of such exacting and diverse subjects as telecommunications, electronic scoreboards, track and field instruments, image (in which the Grupo de Diseño Barcelona-92 will play a very important role, directing the signposting of Olympic installations and areas, publicity, promotion, posters, lithographs and embellishing the city), town-planning, ceremonies (the itinerary of the Olympic Flame, opening ceremonies, proclamations of winners, the closing ceremony and flags) and youth camps.

The press and publications: One of the most relevant aspects of the Olympics is, undoubtedly, the press. Within this we include not only the written and electronic press, but also the publications, audio-visual media and data-banks which must be open to consultation from any country by those who have established the indispensable prior contact with the COJO.

The publications must follow a precise presentation calendar, showing the personification of Spain, cultivating interest and keeping the world informed about the successive phases of organization. The publications programme must be many-hued: as a minimum it should amply surpass the mark of three hundred titles, printing many millions of copies. In order to carry this out, the technical collaboration of most of the ministries as well as that of the Generalitat of Catalunya and the Town Council of Barcelona will be necessary. To this effect, from the moment the city is designated as the seat of the Olympics on, the COJO will have to create a press cabinet which, starting with a nucleus of two, could well reach a total of twenty-five by June and July, 1992.

The quantity and diversity of the publications will take in a wide range because, in addition to the articles prior to the Olympic event, the following will be published: the programme, guidebooks, rulebooks, press guides, information brochures, lists of participants, athletes' guides, traffic guidelines, spectators' guides, guides of the cultural Olympiad, competition calendars, timetables, maps, the itinerary of the Olympic Flame, itineraries for visitors, pocket encylopedias of the Olympic Games, daily results, etc.

All the information, work materials, communications systems, accreditations and the entire press service complex which are to ease the labour of the approximately 10.000 commentators and technicians will converge at the main press centre. This will be set up at the Palacio de Congresos de Montjuïc which has 30.000 m², workshops, offices, conference halls, a spacious assembly hall, simultaneous interpreting. telexes, banks, a restaurant, parking and so forth. Furthermore, its strategic location greatly eases rapid transport to and from the Olympic and residential centres. Press sub-centres will also be set up in each one of the Olympic areas, above all in those of Montjuïc and Tibidabo. Each one of the installations will have a small auxiliary sub-centre.

Security: It is worthwhile to ask oneself if efficient security measures can be compatible with and not destroy the spirit which inspires the Olympic Games; likewise, if it would be possible to obtain a steadfast cooperation and collaboration from the public and athletes if they had to go through very strict security measures for their own welfare.

Without a doubt, these contradictory factors must be born in mind. The Olympic family desires efficient security measures which do not prevent them from moving about at will. And there are other conditions: the security measures should give security rather than inquietude. Above all, care must be taken that an atmosphere is not created by which the security measures stand out too much nor give rise to a psychological climate unfavourable to accepting the measures which have been adopted. The best way to keep trouble-makers away is not by adopting security measures which run counter to human rights, but rather by letting it be known that an unfaltering and strict security blanket is being maintained.

The strategic points in the city should have a sufficient number of uniformed forces of law and order on hand so the athletes and spectators feel safe. To this effect, the forces of law and order should prepare themselves to respect the principle of discreet and efficient security to the utmost.

The following table

Table 9

SECURITY PERSONNEL ESTIMATE

Olympic installations	Ticket control	Perimeter control	Interior control	Post Surv.	Infor- mation	TOTAL
COJO offices	15	15		10	2	42
Main Olympic Village	75	180	80	20	10	265
Rowers' Olympic Village	25	24	20	6	2	77
Sailers' Olympic Village	25	24	20	6	2	77
Youth camps	25	25	20	6	3	79
Press centre	25	12	20	10	3	70
Radio & TV centre	25	12	20	10	3	70
Stadium	50	50	140		70	310
Sports centres	15	20	30		15	80
Swimming pool	15	20	30		15	80
20 competition points	70 people per point					1,400
50 training points	20 people per point					1,000
OLYMPIC INSTALLATIONS TOTAL						3,550
SECURITY OF PARTICIPANTS & PUBLIC						
Athletes and reporters' transport: 400 coaches × 4 people per coach						1,600
VIP escorts: 300 VIPs × 4 people per VIP						1,200
City surveillance reinforcements: 350 pairs × 3 shifts						2,100
SECURITY OF PARTICIPANTS & PUBLIC TOTAL						4,900
SURVEILLANCE OF STRATEGIC POINTS						
Hotels: 15 hotels × 10 people × 3 shifts						450
Airport, port and stations						800
Other points of interest: 20 points × 10 people × 3 shifts						600
STRATEGIC POINTS TOTAL						1,850
ENTRY POINTS & CIRCULATION						
Airport arrivals						50
Station arrivals						50
Border arrivals						50
Traffic to installations outside Barcelona						500
Traffic during marathon, walking, cycling etc. races						500
City traffic reinforcements						500
ENTRY POINTS & CIRCULATION TOTAL						1,650
RESERVES (15 % of the total)						1,900
PERSONNEL TRAINING MONITORS (1 per 100 people)						150
SECURITY PERSONNEL TOTAL						14,000

shows the estimate made about the security personnel required for the holding of the Olympic Games in Barcelona. Together with the proposed technical measures, they will form an efficient security blanket.

Sports: The Olympics rise above their purely athletic significance; nevertheless, it must be stressed that their fundamental raison d'être lies in the competitions of the twenty-three sports in the Olympic programme. The preparation and running of this top-level sports mission has of prime importance the assessment, collaboration and technical assistance of the different Sports Federations in each field. The Spanish Federations of the twenty-three Olympic specialities and the members of the Spanish Olympic Committee should participate to the nth degree – as they are already doing in this phase of candidacy – since this will guarantee a technical and sports organization of the highest standing. As a matter of fact, the Spanish Federations have had a valuable and acknowledged experience in running international competitions as is shown by the circumstance that between 1982 and 1986 they will have organized four very noteworthy world championships; namely, Football, Cycling, Swimming and Basketball.

The Olympic Village: The planning and design of the Olympic Village and of the complementary villas represent one of the most vital headings for a guaranteed success in the Games as the triumphs of the athletes largely depend on their contentedly enjoying this sporting event.

The Olympic teams will be accommodated under a standard of comfort – both in the building structures as well as the services offered – appropiate for athletes who consider excessive luxuries as being innecessary and even inadequate. The Olympic Village should not be viewed from a merely materialistic point of view. It should be capable of creating a harmonious atmosphere for athletes who represent all races and beliefs: So much so that we have proposed a symbolic yet significant ceremony of twinning the Olympic Village with all the cities in the world.

The athletes should feel, as has already been mentioned, at home – surrounded by their own world. The role of the COJO in this consists of providing the Village with whatever material and even inmaterial surroundings that help to create the desired climate. The sportsmen should find warmth and courtesy; it must be remembered that they will spend many hours in the Village and ought to consequently be provided with pastimes and entertainments in accordance to their tastes. As a part of this, it would be convenient if the surroundings and services were such that the athletes would not want to leave the Village during their stay at the Games, as that would somewhat complicate the work of the security forces.

Cultural activities: Although the motive of the Olympic Games is directly related to sports, the cultural and artistic aspects also occupy a highlighted spot in their organization. "The Olympics", as Baron Pierre de Coubertin remarked, "not only have the extolling of muscular force as their mission, they are artistic and intellectual as well and should progressively add to these aspects".

After an unsuccessful attempt to produce a cultural programme as a part of the whole Olympic Festival in the London Games of 1908, this idea gradually gained in strength with the introduction of literary and artistic competitions. The IOC decided to modify their rules in 1952, giving each organizing committee the right to compile a cultural programme on its own.

It is obvious that Barcelona, with its history and tradition, is in good shape to offer a complete programme with a wide range of fields. Its numerous museums and innumerable showrooms and galleries can successfully meet the challenge of a rigorous examination; moreover, there are many varied and spacious places that can be adapted for special exhibitions.

The magnificent Palau de la Musica, not to mention the many other concert halls and auditoriums, can house any symphonic music event with the greatest dignity. The Gran Teatro del Liceo could once again prove to be a suitable stage for opera and ballet. The theatres of the city, most notably the open air Greek Theatre on Montjuïc as well as many other scenic and tried and proven settings, could stage theatrical shows.

Yet all these possibilities – united with handicrafts, folkloric events and simple entertainment – and all these installations should not be a lifeless shell but rather a tool for the preparation of a cultural programme with no other limitation than imagination itself. In this way, the world can be presented with an unforgettable image of Spain, Catalunya and Barcelona.

FINANCES

Initial points

In previous sections an exhaustive inventory has been established of those Sports Facilities, Areas and Systems necessary for the optimal development of the Olympic Games, which for this purpose will entail some type of investment, relatively low in a fair number of cases already in operation, and very high in others which at present exist only on paper.

This diversity of situations makes it indispensable to make an effort at both temporal and conceptual delimitation, in order to determine which investments are specifically imputable to the Games.

Temporal delimitation is easy in so far as a clear-cut date of reference is available: that of proclamation of the host-city. Therefore, work detailed in the inventory which has been completed by this date, or work in progress the continuance of which does not depend on the financial contribution of the Comité Organizador de los Juegos Olímpicos (COJO-Olympic Games Organizing Committee) will not be considered nor included in the accounting for the purpose of determining the investment cost of the Olympic Games. It should be understood that these investments are fully justified independently of their attribution to the Games.

Conceptual delimitation is more complex, above all if one accepts without reserve the version according to which the organization of the Games would not give rise to modifications in the Investment Programmes of the sectors of the Public Administration involved.

What is certain is that from the Olympic point of view, some actions will have to be reconsidered or revised, with inevitable repercussions to the budgets. In fact there are differences between the view which contemplates holding the Games and that which does not, and these differences affect to a greater or lesser extent the content of certain projects as well as their completion dates.

On the basis of these considerations, and independently of the agent or agents who will eventually undertake or share in the execution and financing of each project, for the purpose of determining the total cost of the Games the following will be accounted for as investments:

a) All those affecting facilities –sports, press and accomodation– included under the heading Facilities and not excluded on the basis of temporal delimitation. Exception is made of Accomodation facilities which it is anticipated will be undertaken in principle by the private sector, since in this case adscription to the Games is purely accidental. However, as non-income yielding investments (connected mainly with security requirements), the equivalent of 5 % of the total cost assumed by the private sector has been accounted for as an investment cost of the Games. Logically, rent costs, which increase Organization costs but not investment costs, are considered apart.

b) Those affecting Areas, in so far as they are involved by the location in their interior of Facilities included in the previous point. This point comprises all those listed under the heading Areas, including those affecting facilities imputed to the private sector, with the exception of those excluded on the basis of temporal delimitation.

By applying the criteria of temporal and conceptual delimitation explained above to the entirety of the actions contained under the headings Facilities and Areas, the total investment cost imputable to the Games is obtained, distributed as follows amongst the different sections:

(In millions of pesetas)	
Sports installations	13,965
Training installations	4,010
Press installations	1,520
Lodging installations	942
Undertakings in areas	22,019
	42,456

Their distribution amongst the diverse investing agents has been guided by different considerations, for only thus can a fair distribution of the required financing be achieved. Basically the following have been taken into account: scope of service, public or private ownership, level of post-Games utilization, whether or not new constructions or simply adaptations and improvements had been planned, and finally, the economic capacity of the appropriate investor.

In the application to each specific case of these guidelines, there has been a tendency to accentuate the contribution quota of the COJO, particularly in respect of sports facilities, on the understanding that this is required by a realistic approach. Thus, the contribution quota of the COJO in each of the sections is as follows:

	(Millions Ptas.)	% total
Competition sports installations	7,920	57
Training installations	2,968	74
Press installations	975	64
Lodgings installations	942	5
Undertakings in areas	10,340	47

The COJO, for example, takes on the entire investment in those facilities specific to the Games (Olympic Stadium and Palace) and in those which combine a supramunicipal service network and a great capacity for image transmission. These are conditioned by requirements of a technical nature which would be fulfilled with difficulty if the Games were not held. It is not open to doubt that their existence will strengthen Spain's future possibilities for hosting high-level competitions. The COJO also assumes 100 %, save few exceptions, of the costs of remodelling and improving public or privately-owned facilities, in so far as such work is aimed at fulfilling Olympic requirements. However in cases where the improvement to be effected is considerable, or with new construction, the cost is equally distributed at 50 % as a general rule. The determining factor in the establishment of this percentage is the fact that after the Games the facilities in question will serve as municipal sports facilities (or district facilities in the case of Barcelona city).

Table 10	TOTAL EXPENDITURES (1987-1992) DISTRIBUTED BY AGENTS (in millions of 1983 ptas.)					
CONCEPT	Gen./C	M.B./C	OM/C	Priv./C	COJO	TOTAL
Sports installations (competitions)	375	1,376	350	3,944	7,920	13,965
Sports installations (training)	175	437	0	430	2,968	4,010
Ancillary installations (press)	275	130	140	0	975	1,520
Ancillary installations (lodgings)	0	0	0	18,840	942	19,782
Undertakings in Areas	0	4,116	7,563	0	10,340	22,019
TOTAL	825	6,059	8,053	23,214	23,145	61,296
Periods						
1987-89	600	3,976	4,606	9,845	1,655	20,682
1990-92	225	2,083	3,447	13,369	21,490	40,614
Pro memoria 1983-86						
Sports installations		5,110		200	0	5,310
Ancillary installations		0		0	0	0
Undertakings in Areas		12,645		0	0	12,645
TOTAL		17,755		200	0	17,955

Table 10 Below details the distribution amongst agents of the total investment cost imputable to the Olympic Games. This table is the result of the application of the criteria and considerations explained above. The keys employed to designate the different investing agents are as follows: GEN/C Generalitat-Convenio (Generalitat of Catalonia-Agreement); MB/C Municipio de Barcelona-Convenio (City of Barcelona-Agreement); OM/C Otros Municipios-Convenio (Other Towns-Agreement); Priv./C Sector Privado-Convenio (Private Sector-Agreement); COJO Comité Organizador Juegos Olímpicos (Olympic Games Organizing Committee).

The intention of the addition of Agreement is to safeguard the option, very usual in investments in sports and facilities conditioning, of distributing financing amongst different levels of the Public Administration. In the specific case in question, the Agreement may make possible the financial participation (by means of capital transfers or subsidies) of the Provincial Delegation of Barcelona, the Metropolitan Corporation of Barcelona and the Generalitat of Catalonia, to the benefit mainly of Other Towns, and to a lesser degree, of the City of Barcelona.

Definition of the financing model

The financing model cannot be designed ignoring the exceptional nature of the Olympic Games and the consequent need to take advantage of the experience of other host-cities and countries. Therefore, considerations of proximity in time and/or sociopolitical affinity justify the special attention paid to Munich-72 and Montreal-76, without forgetting almost obligatory reference to Los Angeles-84, in so far as sufficient data are available.

Background

Perhaps the most important conclusions to be drawn from the analysis of previous Olympic experiences are the following: firstly, that in no case were taxes –that is coercive measures– resorted to as a specific source of financing; and secondly, that a balancing character is in fact acquired by the contributions of the Public Administration, which are materialized either by increasing as necessary their initial quota of participation or by combining this formula with the assumption of the final deficit.

On the other hand, the different level of utilization in each case of the diverse sources of revenue is explained in relation to the socio-cultural customs of each country as well as by the effort required by the organization of the Games measured in terms of the respective Gross National Product (GNP). In relation to this last point, Tables 11 and 12 are certainly illustrative.

Table 11

REFERENCE DATA
(The year prior to the holding of the Games)

HEADQUARTERS	Population Millions of inhabitants	GNP Milliards of nat. currency	GNP per capita in nat. currency
Munich 1972			
W. Germany	61,3	759,7	12.400
Bavaria	10,6		11.800
Greater Munich	3,4		
Munich city	1,3		
Montreal 1976			
Canada	23,2	165,4	7.180
Quebec	6,2		
Greater Montreal	2,8		
Montreal city	1,1		
Los Angeles 1984			
USA (*)	234,5	3.278	13.980
California (**)	23,7		
Greater Los Angeles	7,5		
Los Angeles city	3,0		
Barcelona 1992 (*)			
Spain	38,1	22.481	590.000
Catalunya	6,0	4.406	734.379
Greater Barcelona	3,1	2.140	690.300
Barcelona city	1,7	1.318	775.450

(*) Corresponding to 1983 (estimated)
(**) Corresponding to 1980

Table 12

INDICATORS OF ECONOMIC EFFORT

HEADQUARTERS	Total expenditure (Millions of nat. currency)	State		Metropol. Area or Equivalent		City	
		Cost per inhabitant	By thousandths on the cost related to the GNP per capita in the year prior to the Games	Annual cost per inhabitant (*)	By thousandths on the cost related to the GNP per capita in the year prior to the Games	Annual cost per inhabitant (*)	By thousandths on the cost related to the GNP per capita in the year prior to the Games
Munich 1972	1,972	32	2,6	145	11,7	380	31,0
Montreal 1976	1,763	76	10,6	157	22,1	400	56,0
Los Angeles 1984	435,0	2	0,13	14,5	1,0	36	2,6
Barcelona 1992 (**)	88,190	2,314	3,9	7,112	10,3	12,969	16,7

Notes:

(*)   Four-year period prior to the Games.

(**) Corresponding to 1983.

Table 11, in respect of the above-mentioned Olympic host-cities, brings together those macromagnitudes which we consider indispensable for placing the Games, in each case, in their exact context. In Table 12 these magnitudes are related to the total cost of the Games, in order to obtain indicators of apparent effort.

Leaving aside Los Angeles-84, which for our purposes does not constitute a valid reference, the organization of the Olympic Games in Barcelona, were they to be held in 1984, would entail for Spain an apparent effort almost three times less than that of Canada for Montreal-76, and approximately 50 % higher than that of the Federal Republic of Germany for Munich-72.

If the host-city itself, rather than the State, is taken as the frame of reference, the situation of Barcelona would compare favourably with Munich and Montreal. And the same occurs with the spatial reference Metropolitan Area or equivalent. However, discounting revenue from TV rights, in so far as these signify a reduction of the internal financing effort, the comparative position of Spain in respect of that of the German Federal Republic for Munich would noticeably improve, to the point that the respective effort indicators of the two countries would become equal. These data are both categorical and encouraging, especially taking into consideration that from now until 1992 Spain's indicators should evolve positively.

To return to the different level of utilization of sources of revenue observed in each case, having emphasised the explanatory value of the indicator of economic effort, it is quite obligatory to refer to the increasingly important part played by TV rights in the financing of the Olympic Games. This can be clearly seen in Tables 13 and 14 which reflect respectively the financing structures and the evolution as TV rights in the different locations.

Table 13

SOURCES OF INCOME
(In % of the total expenditure)

	Munich 1972	Montreal 1976	Moscow 1980	L.A. 1984	Barcelona 1992
Coins	36,4	6,2	7,6	(4)	3,4
Lotteries	22,2	19,8 y 13,3 (2)	42,7		10,9 (5)
Other (1)	10,6	5,0 y 34,4 (3)	36,0	106,0	68,8
Contribution from the public administration	30,8	21,3	13,7		16,9
TOTAL	100,0	100,0	100,0	106,0	100,0 (6)

Notes:

(1) Includes TV rights, stamps, admission receipts, sports fees, assignments of licences.

(2) Realized post-Games, in accordance with deficit financing programme.

(3) Realized post-Games, in accordance with deficit financing programme. Issuing entirely from a surtax on tobacco consumption.

(4) Given that at the present (Sept. 83) the initial decision of not using this recourse has not been reconsidered, there is no forecast. Nevertheless, taking notice of the surtaxes and minting programme which were fixed, the income under this heading could be substantial.

(5) Includes the contribution from football pools.

(6) Base for the estimate: 88.190 million pesetas.

Certainly, the projection of the evolutionary tendency followed by revenue from TV rights, as graph H shows emphatically, could enable the Games to be financed with external resources, obtained by transfers, a substantial part of the formation process of share capital, over a period of six years.

While we shall refrain from analyzing here the future possibilities of this source of financing, we cannot resist reproducing (Table 15) the hypothetical figures resulting from the extension to past Olympic Games of the level of revenue from TV rights corresponding to Los Angeles-84.

Table 14			
GROSS INCOME FOR TV RIGHTS			
HEADQUARTERS	Total (Millions of $ at current value)	USA TV contribution (In %)	Total (Millions of 1972 $)
Munich 1972	18,3	73,8	18,3
Montreal 1976	31,7	72,6	26,5
Moscow 1980	100,8	84,3	57,7
Los Angeles 1984 (Forecast)	285,0	78,9	143,3

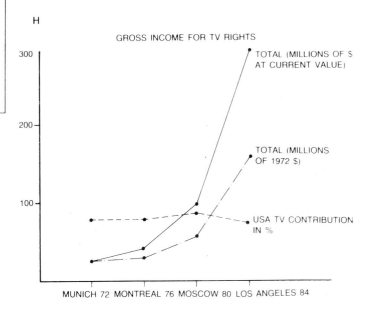

GROSS INCOME FOR TV RIGHTS

Table 15					
		SIMULATION OF SETTINGS (November 1983)			
	1	2	3		
HEADQUARTERS	(*) Actualized total expenditures	(**) Net income L.A. TV rights 1984 as in distribution agreement	Gross income L.A. TV rights 1984	% 3/1	% real contribution
	(In millions of national currency)				
Munich 1972	3,390	766	561	16,5	1,0
Montreal 1976	3,360	352	258	7,7	1,4
Los Angeles 1984	435	285	152	35,0	—
Barcelona 1992 (***)	88,190	44,000	32,500	36,8	—

Notes:
(*) According to respective consumer price indices.
(**) Exchange rates in force on 8/11/83.
(***) Forecast made in November 1983.

The aim is to bring into relief the notable decrease in the internal economic effort which would have been involved for Munich, reproducing exactly the historical experience of 1972 with the sole variation – apart from logically updating costs– of replacing the revenue from TV rights received in 1972 by the revenue from such rights calculated on the basis of Los Angeles-84. In the case of Montreal the impact would be smaller, but nonetheless appreciable.

It should also be observed that, even operating with a hypothesis which looking ahead to 1992 could be regarded as extremely conservative, the level of TV revenue for Los Angeles would make it possible to cover 36.8 % of the estimated total cost of the organization of the Olympic Games in Barcelona.

To conclude this section, it is of interest to note the constant presence in Olympic Games revenue of that derived, generally via surtaxes on returns, from the issue of commemorative coins and stamps. We see in this not only a source of revenue, but also a method of fomenting the promotion of the Games and perpetuating their memory, as well as a reponse to the expectations of the increasingly important collective interested in philately and numismatics. This being the case, Barcelona-92 must not disappoint in this respect.

Operational principles

From the foregoing analyses and reflections are derived the operative principles and guidelines which shape our proposed model of financing of the Olympic Games, Barcelona-92. The objective is to achieve the highest possible level of selffinancing, adopting for this purpose a strategy of open and flexible negotiation, centered on the following points:

a) Maximum diversification of the sources of financing, in line with previous Olympic experiences, with the express exclusion of those having the nature of taxation.
b) To resist the temptation to exert excessive pressure on those sources of finance which theoretically are the most accessible.
c) To link the contribution of the State Administration to the profits attributable to the holding of the Games and, more specifically, to the increase in tax revenue and budget resources derived from such revenue.
d) To take special care with negotiations with the Treasury and, very particularly, the schedule of revenue-generating contractual negotiations.
e) To foment the collaboration of private enterprise in all areas where this is viable.

In reality, the objective is to arrive at an operative programme halfway between the experiences of Munich and Los Angeles. As of this moment in time, and from a realist position, we understand that no other approach is possible.

Revenue programme

First of all, it must be pointed out that the assessment of the Investment Programmes, in each of its sections, has been carried out in 1983 pesetas for the purpose of maintaining homogeneity of treatment with the relevant areas of work. In addition, and as a working hypothesis, the point of departure is zero growth of the GNP during the period 1984-1992. This by way of an additional measure to accentuate that we are dealing with a minimum hypothesis of the revenue resulting from the application of the programme.

For purposes of systematisation we shall distinguish two major types of revenue: revenue whose negotiation process depends entirely on the COJO, the only limitations being those derived from the Olympic Charter, and revenue for which the authorisation and cooperation of the Government is required, and upon the produce of which the capacity for negotiation of the COJO has scarcely any influence.

Within the first group it is important to distinguish revenue which is the result of considerations (full revenue) and that which does not have this nature, or only in very diluted form (share in revenue). Within the second group we must distinguish transferts and subsidies from revenue which does not involve actual budget transfers strictly speaking, and revenue which requires budget transfers.

Following this outline we shall now proceed to summarise the proposed revenue programme, which, in so far as it is the result of the application of a previously defined financing model, represents one of various possible alternatives.

Full COJO revenue

Gate Takings. Revenue under this heading is calculated at 2,450 million pesetas (1983), from forecasted sales of 3,500,000 tickets at an average price of 700 pesetas. This average price has been estimated from the range of prices current in Spain for national competitions, and is perfectly consistent in terms of economic effort (1.18 per thousand of income per capita) with the precedents of Munich (1.3 per thousand) and Montreal (1.2 per thousand).

For the moment we shall not enter into details of the management of revenue under this heading, although it is indeed opportune to note the expediency of retaining certain special features put into practice in Los Angeles: the admission of applications for reservations two years in advance, upon payment of 10 % of the price of the ticket, and the issue of a limited number of preferential season tickets at a price of 25,000 dollars allowing entry to two events per day.

Participants' Quotas. It is hoped that these will contribute a total of 1,200 million pesetas (1983), for 300,000 days' stays made by 15,000 persons between participants and companions. The average revenue per day is calculated at 4,000 pesetas, lower than the 35 dollars established by the Los Angeles Organizing Committee.

Programmes, posters, lithographs. The expected revenue is of a testimonial nature: 150 million pesetas (1983). Of this amount, 100 millions are imputed to the sale of programmes, and it is estimated that only 10 % of publication costs will be covered, if the experience of Montreal is reproduced. The estimated revenue from the sale of posters and lithographs may easily be exceeded if, as is foreseeable, the collaboration of well-known artists is obtained. Nevertheless, it should not be forgotten that the essential purpose is not to obtain revenue but to promote the Olympic Games.

Assignment of Licences. This heading includes revenue from the assignment of licences for the utilization of Olympic emblems and symbols in the manufacture and marketing of products, including medals and, naturally, the mascot of the Games. It is envisaged as feasible to obtain under this heading a net revenue of approximately 2,000 million pesetas, of which 700, also net, would stem from the assignment of licences to foreign countries.

TV Rights. Revenue under this heading, after deduction of the IOC quota is estimated at 32,500 million pesetas (1983). This has been sufficiently discussed under the heading. "Definition of the Financing Project."

Services. Revenue under this heading is obtained from: - the utilization of premises and equipment by those radio-television channels which are making unilateral programmes: 1,500 million pesetas (1983). This figure corresponds to the revenue obtained by TVE (Spanish Television) for the World Cup-82, and is therefore extremely conservative. - the exclusive utilization of premises within the facilities for the Press, by same: 100 million pesetas (1983). - the sale of tickets for cultural events envisaged during the Olympic games: 30 million pesetas.

Interest and Other Financial Revenue. This is estimated at 2,500 pesetas and its realization depends on the actual flow of revenue and expenditure confirming the following Treasury forecast:

Table 16	Income (including interest)	Expenses
1987	3,05	2,00
1988	2,10	2,20
1989	3,80	2,30
1990	11,10	9,20
1991	24,25	22,60
1992	27,70	34,75
1993	1,00	0,20
	73,25	73,25

The interest has been calculated at the rate of 15 %, not unusual in such cases, especially if it is borne in mind that financial entities are able to obtain far from negligible returns. In this respect it would be worth studying the possibility of reaching an agreement with a bank or group of banks for the purpose of creating an Olympic division within them, thus strengthening the revenue under this heading.

Share in Revenue

Lotteries. The lottery programme proposed is as follows: three ordinary draws of the National Lottery are to be converted into extraordinary draws, spaced at suitable intervals, on exactly the same terms as those which were duly authorised to the benefit of the Royal Organizing Committee of the World Cup-82. Considering the slowing down of growth observed in the sale of National Lottery tickets since 1980, our point of departure is that the COJO's share will reach 700 million pesetas per draw (the Royal Organizing Committee of the World Cup-82 received 638 million). Total revenue from this source would therefore be 2,100 million pesetas (1983).

Football Pools. The revenue programme under this heading contemplates the establishment of an extraordinary surcharge of 0.50 centimes on each bet placed, on terms similar to those established by Royal Decree 1635/1980 of 18 July, in favour of the Royal Organizing Committee of the World Cup 1980. The decree would be in force for six seasons, from the time the host-city is proclaimed to the closing session of the Games. The revenue would be shared equally between the COJO and the Spanish Olympic Committee, which in this way would be able to attend to a specific programme for the promotion of Olympic sports. The number of bets which will be placed during the 1983-84 season is estimated to be, on the low side, 5,400 million (4,900 were placed in 82-83); the COJO would therefore obtain 1,350 million pesetas, thereby calculating its total revenue at 8,100 million pesetas (1983).

Coins. The revenue programme under this heading contemplates the COJO's sharing, by way of surtax, in the return on the issue of gold and silver coins, legal tender, along the lines of what has become customary in recent Olympiads. Naturally the approval of the Government and especially of the Ministry of Finance will be required. The corresponding Royal Decree could easily specify the characteristics of the issues (number of coins, alloy, inscription and design of obverse and reverse), and the maximum circulation of the coins should be established in the National Budget.

To obtain the 3,000 million pesetas proposed in this programme, would mean, for example, that on the hypothesis of minimum surtax, the total value of the issues and selling prices, including tax, should reach 55,000 million pesetas. Their placement would require an average expenditure per family unit equivalent to 0.3 % of its disposable income for 1983, which would rise to 1.2 % if only those family units with a disposable income higher than 1,700,000 pesetas were taken into consideration. The feasibility of the proposed programme would be strengthened if the possibilities of foreign markets, according to the experience of Moscow-80, were considered.

Stamps. The revenue obtainable by the COJO under this heading is valued at 1,000 million pesetas (1983), on the basis of a surtax established as a percentage of the face value of special issues of stamps, sets and postcards, which would constitute the Olympic philatelic programme. Of these 1,000 million pesetas a minimum of 100 million could accrue from commercialisation in foreign markets.

Transfers and Subsidies

From the private sector. Under this subheading, from which the obtention of 3,000 million pesetas is foreseen, only financial transfers contributed by Sponsors have been quantified. Within the revenue programme, this is the item which is most markedly a target figure, in so far as the only significant data available are those pertaining to Los Angeles-84.

From the public sector. This heading includes all revenue proceeding from the Public Sector, by means of transfers or subsidies. Nevertheless, in practice, we have confined ourselves to considering and therefore evaluating what in our judgement should be contributed by the State. We are thus taking for granted, for reasons of fairness, that it should make a financial contribution to the organization of the Games, in so far as these generate external nationwide economies, difficult to quantify in some cases (international promotion and diffusion). For this reason, the financing model adopted advocates linking the State's contribution exclusively to the increase in its tax revenue, in so far as this may be specifically attributable to the Games. It should be observed that on the basis of this concept the participation of the State as an investing agent has been excluded. That is, the State's contribution to the Overall Games Budget and, more specifically, to the COJO's Preliminary Budget is conditioned by the manifestation of tangible and quantifiable profits. And this is entirely independent of the balance presented by the COJO upon termination of its functions. According to the method of calculation followed, the forecast of 8,000 million pesetas under this heading should be regarded as extremely conservative.

Sale of Assets

To forecast the revenue to be obtained under this heading, the general criterion has been to consider that the sale of assets will generate a recovery in no case higher than 50 % of the cost of their adquisition, which will determine a revenue of 5,620 million pesetas.

The Games Budget

The budget is structured on two levels: the COJO's preliminary budget, which comprises only revenue and expenditure imputable to the COJO itself, and the overall Games budget, which is the result of adding to the former the direct investments of the Public Administration.

Table 17
INITIAL BUDGET OF THE ORGANIZING COMMITTEE
(In milliards of pesetas)
NOVEMBER 1983

EXPENDITURES

I. *Organization of the Games*		42,64
I.1. Personnel	10,26	
I.2. Services and purchased materials	21,15	
I.3. Setting up installations	11,23	
II. *Installations (Share of contribution)*		12,80
II.1. Competition sports grounds	7,92	
II.2. Training sports grounds	2,97	
II.3. Ancillary (Press)	0,97	
II.4. Ancillary (Lodgings)	0,94	
III. *Undertakings in Areas*		10,34
III.1. Basic expenses	0,00	
III.2. Modernization	10,34	
IV. *Unforeseen expenses*		7,47
TOTAL		73,25

Pro memoria
Share of direct public administration investments in: Installations and Undertakings in Areas — 14,94

OVERALL ESTIMATED BUDGET OF THE OLYMPIC GAMES — 88,19

Table 18
INITIAL BUDGET OF THE ORGANIZING COMMITTEE
(In milliards of pesetas)
NOVEMBER 1983

INCOME

I. *Organizing Committee Income*		42,43
I.1. Admission Fees	2,45	
I.2. Lodgings in the Olympic Village	1,20	
I.3. Programmes, Posters & Lithographs	0,15	
I.4. Cession of Licences	2,00	
I.5. TV Rights	32,50	
I.6. Contributed Services	1,63	
I.7. Interest & Other Revenue	2,50	
II. *Share in Revenue*		14,20
II.1. Lotteries	2,10	
II.2. Football Pools	8,10	
II.3. Coins	3,00	
II.4. Stamps	1,00	
III. *Transfers & Grants*		11,00
III.1. Private Sector	3,00	
III.2. Public Sector	8,00	
IV. *Sale of Assets*		5,62
TOTAL		73,25

Pro memoria
Countervalue of the share of direct investments by public administrations — 14,94

OVERALL ESTIMATED BUDGET OF THE OLYMPIC GAMES — 88,19

In accordance with the basic hypotheses employed in order to elaborate the various sections of expenditure-costs (Organization, Facilities and Areas) and of revenue (Revenue Programme), the preliminary Olympic Games budget has been drawn up and presented in 1983 pesetas.

In respect of the revenue statement, we must once more insist on the markedly conservative nature of the figures involved. In this respect, it may be affirmed that the revenue budget corresponds to the least favourable situation of those reasonably foreseeable. For this reason, it is practically certain that reality will confirm, at least, the total revenue budgeted for, while at the same time, the existence is clearly shown of a financial capacity more than sufficient for carrying out the organization of the Games.

Preliminary Budget of the COJO

The COJO's preliminary budget reaches a total of 73,250 million pesetas, with equal revenue and expenditure. It is the heading Incidental Expenses, which represents approximately 10 % of the total, that balances the budget.

As may be observed, the weightiest item under the Statement of Expenditure corresponds to the Organization of the Games, which represents 58 % of the total. Within this percentage, half corresponds to Purchase of Property and Services, that is, almost 30 % of the total budget. The other half is almost equally distributed between personnel costs and the equipping of facilities.

The remaining 40 % is distributed amongst the quotas of participation of the COJO in facilities (18 %), actions in Areas (14 %) and incidental expenses (10 %). Of the 18 % corresponding to facilities, the most important item is competition sports facilities, which represents two thirds.

Within actions in Areas, a distinction has been made between basic costs and costs of conditioning. Obviously, in view of its nature the COJO does not participate in the financing of the basic costs; on the other hand it undertakes 100 % of the costs of conditioning.

In respect of Revenue, Full Revenue totals 58 %; prominent under this heading is the revenue from TV rights, which accounts for three quarters of the total. The remaining items are distributed around similar percentages, in no case exceeding 3.5 %.

The relative weight of the second heading, Share in Revenue, is almost 20 % of the total budget. Prominent under this heading are Football Pools, with 57 %, followed by Coins, with 21 %.

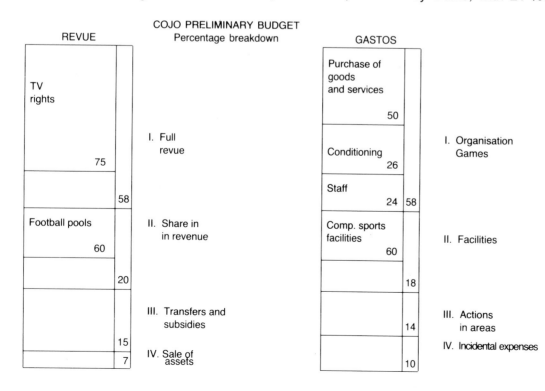

Transfers and Subsidies accounts for 15 % of the total revenue budget, with those from the public sector and more specifically from the State having the most weight.

Finally, Sale of Assets accounts for somewhat more than 7 % of the total revenue budget.

The comparison, in terms of structure, between Revenue and Expenditure, of which a graphic version is included, allows certain interesting aspects to be underlined. Thus, it is important to point out the correspondence between full revenue and organization costs. Each of these accounts for approximately 58 % of its respective total budget. That is, the organization of the Olympic Games is self-financing thanks mainly to revenue from TV rights, which alone cover three quarters of the total organization costs. From this it may be inferred that a large part of these costs are covered by transfers from abroad.

If Share in Revenue is added to Full Revenue, the total amount covers more than sufficiently the aggregate of organization costs and the quota of participation in facilities. That is, that which, from a more restrictive perspective in the imputation of costs to the COJO, would have transformed the strict cost of the organization of the Olympic games.

Overall Games Budget

As was previously pointed out, to obtain the overall Games budget, it is necessary to add to the COJO's preliminary budget the quota of direct investment assumed by the subcentral public administration (as long as the State does not participate) in facilities and actions in Areas, a total of 14,940 million pesetas.

The total figure of the overall Games Budget is, therefore, 88,190 million pesetas.

The direct contribution of the subcentral public administration, therefore, accounts for 17 % of the overall Games Budget, and is materialised in the form of direct investment. In respect of its amount, it must be pointed out that this is not very relevant compared with the investment capacity of these public entities. By way of illustration, from the recent study apropos of this project made by the Finances and Planning Services Management of the Metropolitan Corporation of Barcelona, entitled "Evolution of resources and potential investment of the towns of the MCB area (1983-1992)", we reproduce the following paragraph from the chapter "Conclusions":

"The ordinary available resources of the towns of the MCB during the entire period 1983-1992 would be, on the minimum supposition, 886,092.05 million pesetas and on the maximum supposition, 1,151,321,8 million 1992 pesetas. If it is assumed that the total investment of the towns –financed by ordinary recourses, burden of debts, subsidies and special levies– is in the same proportion as now (30.74 % of ordinary resources of 1982), then the volume of total investments to be made in the period 1983-1992 would reach a figure between 272,384.8 and 353,916,3 million 1982 pesetas. The potential investment could be even higher on the maximum supposition, if we take into account the greater rigour in ordinary expenditure, which would contribute to increasing the available margin in order to increase ordinary revenue."

It should be observed that the comparison between the 14,940 million pesetas in direct public investment registered in the overall Games budget, plus the 17,755 million not registered in the budget as their realisation is envisaged during the period 1983-1986, that is, in total 32,695 million pesetas, and the 272,000 million pesetas of minimum investment capacity estimated for the MCB towns in conjunction for the period 1983-1992, yields a figure of 12 %, which drops to approximately 8 % by deducting from the 32,695 millions that part which foreseeably will be assumed by the MCB itself, the Provincial Delegation of Barcelona and the Generalitat of Catalonia.

Which permits us to conclude, categorically, that the organization of the 1992 summer Olympic Games will not jeopardize the normal investment process of these public agents.

CHRONOLOGY

January 1981
At the dinner for the announcement of the best Spanish sportsmen of 1980, the Mayor of Barcelona announces to the President of the International Olympic Committee, Juan Antonio Samaranch, his desire to offer Barcelona as the host-city for the 1992 Olympic Games.

May 1981
The Mayor of Barcelona requests the authorization and sponsorship of H.M. King Juan Carlos I for the candidature of Barcelona.

June 1981
The Plenum of the Barcelona City Council votes unanimously in favour of the initiative. The initial project is commissioned.

October 1982
Presentation of "Olympic Games Project, Barcelona 1992, First Approaches", which responds affirmatively to all the basic principles posed.

November 1982
The Major of Barcelona and the Director-General of Sports of the Generalitat of Catalonia present this initial project at the IOC headquarters in Lausanne, to the President Juan Antonio Samaranch.

December 1983
The Spanish Prime Minister, Felipe Gonzalez, communicates to the Mayor of Barcelona, Pasqual Maragall, the total support of his Cabinet for the candidature of Barcelona.

January 1983
Formation of the Steering Committee for the candidature of Barcelona-92.
Creation of the Olympic Office, charged with the preparation, management and execution of all work for the presentation of the candidature.

February 1983
The Metropolitan Corporation of Barcelona accepts the project and all the mayors pertaining to the Corporation give their adherence to the candidature.

June 1983
First Olympic Symposium of Barcelona.

July 1983
Presentation of the bases of the Montjuïc Olympic Ring contest and the pre-selected architects.

December 1983
The Chamber of Commerce, Industry and Shipping and private companies offer contributions to the financing of the candidature.
The Steering Committee approves and presents to the media the "Initial Project for the Candidature of Barcelona-1922".

January 1984

Announcement of the winners of the Montjuïc Olympic Ring contest. The work as a whole is awarded to the team of architects Correa, Milà, Margarit and Buxadé, the construction of the Sports Palace to the Japanese Arata Isozaki, the Stadium to the teams directed by Federico Correa and Vittorio Gregotti, the press sub-centre – future headquarters of the INEF within the framework of the University of Sports, to Ricardo Bofill. The German Richard Weidle is appointed permanent Sports Engineering Consultant.

March 1984

After detailed study, the Spanish Olympic Committee approves the Initial Project Barcelona-1992.
The Sports Council, after receiving favourable reports from the Olympic Sports Federations, passes on the Initial Project to the Government.
The Government, through a meeting of the Council of Ministers, gives its approval and support to the candidature of Barcelona.

April 1984

The Mayor of Barcelona, Pasqual Maragall, and the winning architects sign contracts for the construction of the Montjuïc Olympic Ring.
The Mayor of Barcelona opens the exhibition "Montjuïc Olimpic", of the architectural projects for the Olympic Ring.

May 1984

Contest for the design of the candidature's logo. Contest for the planning project for the requirements of telecommunications and data processing.

June 1984

Second Olympic Symposium of Barcelona.

INDEX OF TEXTS

Summary of the preliminary project of the Candidature of Barcelona for the 1992 Olympic Games.